AMERICA'S CHRISTIAN HERITAGE

AMERICA'S CHRISTIAN HERITAGE

GARY DeMAR

BROADMAN
& HOLMAN
PUBLISHERS

Nashville, Tennessee

0-8054-3032-6

Published by Broadman & Holman Publishers,
Nashville, Tennessee

Dewey Decimal Classification: 973
Subject Heading: UNITED STATES—HISTORY—
RELIGIOUS ASPECTS \ CHRISTIANITY—HISTORY

Unless stated otherwise, Bible citations are from the King James Version. Scripture verses cited as NKJV are from the New King James Version, © 1979, 1980, 1982, Thomas Nelson, Inc., Publishers. Passages cited as NASB are from the New American Standard Bible, © the Lockman Foundation, 1960, 1962, 1963, 1968, 1971, 1972, 1973, 1975, 1977; used by permission.

America's Christian Heritage is adapted from Gary DeMar's
America's Christian History: The Untold Story published by American Vision.
For more information, please contact American Vision,
P.O. Box 220, Powder Springs, GA 30127,
call 1-800-628-9460, or go to www.americanvision.org

1 2 3 4 5 6 7 8 9 10 07 06 05 04 03

CONTENTS

1

AMERICA'S CHRISTIAN HERITAGE: FACT OR FICTION?

When Kirk Fordice, former governor of Mississippi, stated without reservation that "America is a Christian nation,"[1] the response from many bordered on the hysterical. The governor's controversial remarks landed him on CNN. His comments are perceptive and irrefutable. He stated simply:

> Christianity is the predominant religion in America. We all know that's an incontrovertible fact. The media always refer to the Jewish state of Israel. They talk about the Muslim country of Saudi Arabia, of Iran, of Iraq. We all talk about the Hindu nation of India. America is not a nothing country. It's a Christian country.[2]

History is on the side of Governor Fordice, as Terry Eastland, publisher of *The Weekly Standard*, has confirmed after his in-depth study of the history of America. "Protestant Christianity has been our established religion in almost every sense of that phrase. . . . The establishment of Protestant Christianity was one not only of law but also, and far more importantly, of culture. Protestant Christianity supplied the

nation with its 'system of values.'"[3] This statement of historical fact, inscribed into law by the United States Supreme Court, etched into charters and state constitutions, and echoed by presidents and governors for nearly four centuries, clashes with modern-day secular assumptions and the normless ideals of multiculturalism, political correctness, and moral relativism. James Billington, Librarian of Congress, said in a news conference on the opening of the exhibit, "Religion and the Founding of the American Republic," that "the dominant role religion played in the earliest days of this country is largely ignored by media, academics, and others."[4]

The reality of America's Christian roots runs deep and wide throughout the landscape of our nation's history. At every point in our nation's past, America's Christian heritage can be seen at nearly every turn through the voluminous historical records that have been painstakingly preserved. And beyond the proof inscribed in the official story of America, there is the abundant anecdotal evidence that surfaces from every corner of the globe.

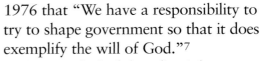

Franklin Delano Roosevelt

In 1931 the U.S. Supreme Court noted that the United States is a Christian nation. In a mid-Atlantic summit with British Prime Minister Winston Churchill in the darkest hours of World War II, President Roosevelt —who had described the United States as "the lasting concord between men and nations, founded on the principles of Christianity"— asked the crew of an American warship to join him in a rousing chorus of the hymn "Onward, Christian Soldiers."

In 1947, writing to Pope Pius XII, President Truman said flatly, "This is a Christian nation."

Nobody argued with any of them.[5]

If any president made such claims today, he would be derided by a hostile press and mocked by an academic elite in the highly charged atmosphere of political correctness that has imbedded itself into discussion forums at every level of our society. So would former presidents Woodrow Wilson and Jimmy Carter. In his famous address, "The Bible and Progress," delivered in Denver, Colorado, on May 7, 1911, President Wilson told his audience that "America was born a Christian nation. America was born to exemplify that devotion to the elements of righteousness which are derived from the revelations of Holy Scripture."[6] As a presidential candidate Jimmy Carter told reporters in June of

Woodrow Wilson

1976 that "We have a responsibility to try to shape government so that it does exemplify the will of God."[7]

A great deal of the editorial savagery leveled against Governor Fordice could have been alleviated if the historical record had been studied in an objective way. But even this would not have been enough. Facts are not the problem. There is often a bias against things Christian. Religion is fine, say the secularists, as long as it remains a private affair and does not spill over into the areas of morality, education, and politics. But this is not the America of history.

WHAT IT IS NOT

The claim that America has a distinct Christian heritage does not mean that every American is now or ever was a Christian. Moreover, it does not mean that either the Church or the State should force people to profess belief in Christianity or attend religious services. Furthermore, a belief in a Christian heritage for America does not mean that non-Christians, and for that matter, dissenting Christians, cannot hold contrary opinions in a climate of a general Christian consensus.

WHAT IT IS

It's one thing to claim that there is no evidence of a Christian heritage for America and prove it. It's another thing to fabricate history to suit one's entrenched presuppositions. An honest study of America's past will show that a majority of Americans shared a common religion and ethic. America's earliest founders were self-professing Christians and their founding documents expressed a belief in a Christian worldview. John Winthrop's sermon aboard the *Arabella* in 1630 is one piece of evidence supporting this historical truth.

John Winthrop

> For the persons, we are a Company professing ourselves fellow members of Christ. . . .
>
> For the work we have in hand, it is by a mutual consent through a special overruling providence, and a more than an ordinary approbation of the Churches of Christ to seek out a place of Cohabitation and Consortship under a due form of Government both civil and ecclesiastical. . . .[8]

Freedom and liberty, ideals cherished by all Americans, were rooted in a biblical moral order. Liberty was not license. Freedom was not the right always to do what one pleased. Winthrop's definition of liberty is far from the modern meaning. As it is usually defined today, liberty is freedom from moral restraints. One is not truly free, according to the contemporary use of the term, if one is bound by any moral code.

A FOREIGNER'S VIEW

In 1831 the French social philosopher Alexis de Tocqueville landed in America to observe the new nation and her institutions. Tocqueville's work was published in two parts at the mid-point of the nineteenth century as *Democracy in America*. It has been described as "the most comprehensive and penetrating analysis of the relationship between character and society in America that has ever been written."[9] His observations on America's moral ideals are revealing and worthy of study.

> The sects that exist in the United States are innumerable. They all differ in respect to the worship which is due to the Creator; but they all agree in respect to the duties which are due from man to man. Each sect adores the Deity in its own peculiar manner, *but all sects preach the same moral law* in the name of God. . . . Moreover, all the sects of the United States are comprised within the great unity of Christianity, and *Christian morality is everywhere the same. . . . [T]here is no country in the world where the Christian religion retains a greater influence over the souls of men than in America.*[10]

Two-hundred years after John Winthrop's sermon aboard the *Arabella*, Tocqueville continued to find in America "an ostensible respect for Christian morality and virtue."[11] This is the substance of a working definition of "Christian America"—the sharing of common moral values that have been shaped with reference to the Bible. "The biblical model of a 'city on a hill,'" to use Winthrop's phrase, "was the relevant goal for political action. Puritan divines called for the establishment of a 'Holy Community,' governed according to standards derived from Christian principles of morality and justice."[12]

Alexis de Tocqueville

THE SUPREME COURT HAS SPOKEN

Associate Justice David J. Brewer

For many Americans, official recognition of anything is found in the Supreme Court. So what has the highest court in the land determined? In 1892, the Supreme Court declared, in the case of *The Church of the Holy Trinity vs. United States,* that America was a Christian nation from its earliest days. After examining a full range of historical documents, Associate Justice David J. Brewer concluded that Americans are "a religious people. This is historically true. From the discovery of this continent to the present hour, there is a single voice making this affirmation." Beginning with Ferdinand and Isabella's commission to Christopher Columbus, through a survey of then current state constitutions, the court concluded:

> There is no dissonance in these declarations. There is a universal language pervading them all, having one meaning; they affirm and reaffirm that this is a religious nation. These are not individual sayings, declarations of private persons: they are organic utterances; they speak the voice of the entire people.

> If we pass beyond these matters to a view of American life as expressed by its laws, its business, its customs and its society, we find everywhere a clear recognition of the same truth. Among other matters note the

Christopher Columbus landing on Island of Guanahani, West Indies

"WE ARE A RELIGIOUS PEOPLE..."

following: The form of oath universally prevailing, concluding with an appeal to the Almighty; the custom of opening sessions of all deliberative bodies and most conventions with prayer; the prefatory words of all wills, "In the name of God, amen"; the laws respecting the observance of the Sabbath, with the general cessation of all secular business, and the closing of courts, legislatures, and other similar public assemblies on that day; the churches and church organizations which abound in every city, town and hamlet; the multitude of charitable organizations existing everywhere under Christian auspices; the gigantic missionary associations, with general support, and aiming to establish Christian missions in every quarter of the globe. These, and many other matters which might be noticed, add a volume of unofficial declarations to the mass of organic utterances that this is a Christian nation.[13]

In 1931, Supreme Court Justice George Sutherland reviewed the 1892 decision and reaffirmed that Americans are a "Christian people." As late as 1952, even the liberal Supreme Court Justice William O. Douglas declared that "we are a religious people and our institutions presuppose a Supreme Being."

In addition to writing the opinion in the *Holy Trinity* case, David Brewer wrote *The United States: A Christian Nation*, a series of lectures that were published in book form in 1905 while he

George Sutherland

was still a member of our nation's highest court.[14] In it, Brewer reiterates the history behind the 1892 *Trinity* case and states clearly that America was founded as a Christian nation, as the following citations from his book indicate:

• "This republic is classified among the Christian nations of the world."

• "In the case of *Holy Trinity Church vs. United States*, 143 U.S. 471, that court, after mentioning various circumstances, add, 'these and many other matters which might be noticed, add a volume of unofficial declarations to the mass of organic utterances that this is a Christian nation.'"

William O. Douglas

• "[W]e constantly speak of this republic as a Christian nation—in fact, as the leading Christian nation in the world. This popular use of the term certainly has significance. It is not a mere creation of the imagination. It is not a term of derision, but has a substantial basis—one which justifies its use."

• "In no charter or constitution is there anything to even suggest that any other than the Christian is the religion of this country. In none of them is Mohammed or Confucius or Buddha in any manner noticed. In none of them is Judaism recognized, other than by way of toleration of its special creed. While the separation

11

of church and state is often affirmed, there is nowhere a repudiation of Christianity as one of the institutions as well as benedictions of society. In short, there is no charter or constitution that is either infidel, agnostic, or anti-Christian. Wherever there is a declaration in favor of any religion, it is of the Christian."

• "You will have noticed that I have presented no doubtful facts. Nothing has been stated which is debatable. The quotations from charters are in the archives of the several States; the laws are on the statute books; judicial opinions are taken from the official reports; statistics from the census publications. In short, no evidence has been presented which is open to question."

• "I could show how largely our laws and customs are based upon the laws of Moses and the teachings of Christ; how constantly the Bible is appealed to as the guide of life and the authority in questions of morals."

David Brewer's conclusion?—"This is a Christian nation." Our study would be incomplete if we did not take the same road that David Brewer and others have taken that led them to this bold and unpopular conclusion. That road will inevitably lead us to the original founding documents of America. The signposts are everywhere present as we let the record speak for itself.

[1] *U.S. News & World Report* (November 30, 1992), 21.

[2] "Mississippi Governor Criticized for 'Christian Nation' Remark," *Dallas/Fort Worth Heritage* (January 1993), 14. Quoted in John W. Whitehead, *Religious Apartheid: The Separation of Religion from American Public Life* (Chicago, IL: Moody Press, 1994), 149.

[3] Terry Eastland, "In Defense of Religious America," *Commentary: A Monthly Publication of the American Jewish Committee* (June 1981), 39–41.

[4] Quoted in Bill Broadway, "One Nation Under God," *The Washington Post* (June 6, 1998), B9.

[5] Larry Witham, "'Christian Nation' Now Fighting Words," *The Washington Times* (November 23, 1992), A1.

[6] The Papers of Woodrow Wilson, ed. Arthur S. Link, 57 vols. (Princeton, NJ: Princeton University Press, 1966), 23:12–20. Quoted in Richard V. Pierard and Robert D. Linder, *Civil Religion and the Presidency* (Grand Rapids, MI: Academie/Zondervan, 1988), 153.

[7] Richard G. Hutcheson, Jr., *God in the White House: How Religion Has Changed the Modern Presidency* (New York: Macmillan, 1988), 1.

[8] John Winthrop (1588-1649), "A Model of Christian Charity," (1630), quoted in Mark A. Noll, ed., *Eerdmans' Handbook to Christianity in America* (Grand Rapids, MI: Eerdmans, 1983), 38.

[9] Robert N. Bellah, et al., *Habits of the Heart: Individualism and Commitment in American Life* (Berkeley, CA: University of California Press, 1985), viii.

[10] Alexis de Tocqueville, *Democracy in America*, 2 vols. (New York: Alfred A. Knopf, 1945), 1:303. Emphasis added.

[11] Tocqueville, *Democracy in America*, 1:305.

[12] A. James Reichley, *Religion in American Public Life* (Washington, DC: The Brookings Institution, 1985), 55.

[13] *Church of the Holy Trinity v. United States.* Argued and submitted January 7, 1892. Decided February 29, 1892. Justice Brewer delivered the opinion of the court.

[14] David J. Brewer, *The United States: A Christian Nation* (Philadelphia, PA: The John C. Winston Company, 1905). The book has been reprinted under the same title by American Vision, P.O. Box 220, Powder Springs, GA 30127.

1

"BY THE PROVIDENCE OF AMIGHTY GOD"

CHRISTIANITY IN COLONIAL AMERICA

Our nation begins not in 1776, but more than one hundred and fifty years earlier. Thirteen colonies with independent governments and intact constitutions were operating at the time the Declaration of Independence was drafted and signed.

The political ideals of those who forged a more unified nation were not developed within a worldview vacuum. Since ideas have consequences, we should expect that the beliefs of the existing colonies would influence the future unified nation. Sadly, however, the truth

American flag with thirteen original colonies represented

about our once robust Christian heritage is being steadily dismantled. The early colonies' reliance on God's providence is nothing more than a faded memory for most Americans. If we are ever to restore what is in danger of being lost, we will need to learn the truth about our nation's history. A look at some of the earliest colonies and their governing charters is a good starting point.

FIRST CHARTER OF VIRGINIA

The earliest efforts at colonization in the seventeenth century followed two main roads—the Jamestown Colony in Virginia (1607) and Plymouth Plantation in Massachusetts (1620).

The London Company adequately planned and financed the expedition to establish the first permanent English colony in America at Jamestown. Similar to all the colonial charters, the First Charter of Virginia emphasizes the Christian character of the purpose of the expedition. Their task was defined "by the providence of Almighty God, . . . to the glory of His Divine Majesty, in propagating of the Christian religion to such people, as yet live in darkness and miserable ignorance of the true knowledge and worship of God."[1]

While the expedition was well financed, those of the Virginia colony were not suitably prepared to handle

Fort at Jamestown

"THE CHRISTIAN RELIGION WAS THE UNDERLYING BASIS ... OF THE VIRGINIA COLONY." —B.F. MORRIS

the hardships that would confront them. Most who made the voyage were gentlemen adventurers. "There were no men with families. There were very few artisans, and none with any experience that would fit them to get a living out of the soil. . . . Of them Captain Smith said, 'A hundred good workmen were worth a thousand such gallants.'"[2] Even so, their Christian faith saw them through periods of despair and trampled hope. The Rev. Robert Hunt—"an honest, religious, and courageous Divine," as described by Captain John Smith—was chaplain of the expedition. Worship services began almost from the hour of landing in May of 1607. "There the first seed for English Christianity on the American continent was sown."[3]

The Jamestown colonists suffered great hardship. At a time when they were nearly out of food, with their original colony down to about fifty from the original 104, God provided sustenance from an unlikely source. Here is how one of the survivors, William Simmonds, describes their situation: "But now was all our provision spent, the sturgeon gone, all helps abandoned, each other expecting the fury of the savages, when God, the patron of all good endeavors, in that desperate extremity, so changed the hearts of the savages that they brought such plenty of their fruits and provision that no man wanted."[4] When the new governor of Jamestown, Lord de La Warr, arrived in 1610, the colony was on the verge of collapse. His first action was to organize a worship service and issue a biblical call for sacrifice and enterprise.

After a thorough study of the Virginia colonial period, B. F. Morris, in his voluminous *Christian Life and Character of the Civil Institutions of the United States*, concluded, "The Christian religion was the underlying basis and the pervading element of all the social and civil institutions of the Virginia colony."[5]

Mayflower Compact

MASSACHUSETTS AND THE MAYFLOWER COMPACT

In the early part of the seventeenth century, England was a country of religious intolerance. Ministers of the Gospel were silenced, imprisoned, or exiled. In 1609, because of persecution, a group of Christians left their village in Scrooby, England, and went to the Netherlands, where they found a fair amount of religious freedom. Led by their pastor, John Robinson, this group

Embarkation of the Pilgrims at Delfthaven, Holland, July 22, 1620

settled in Leyden, Holland, where they formed an English Separatist Church.

After a few years, the English transplants began to be concerned that their children were adopting the Dutch language and customs, while losing sight of their English heritage. In addition, they wanted to live in a society that was thoroughly founded on the Bible, not simply a place where they would have the freedom to go to the church of their choice. These Separatists (Pilgrims) decided to go to the New World, where they could live as Englishmen and in accordance with the Bible.

Unable to finance the trip, the Separatists arranged financial support from a group of English businessmen. These venture capitalists were to receive any profits the colony made in its first seven years. The Pilgrims were also granted permission from the London group of the Virginia Company to settle in Virginia, north of Jamestown. Prior to their departure from Holland, Rev. Robinson called for a solemn fast and then delivered an embarkation sermon as a portion of the flock prepared to depart for American shores:

> I charge you, before God and his blessed angels, that you follow me no further than you have seen me follow the Lord Jesus Christ. The Lord has more truth yet to break forth out of his holy word. I cannot sufficiently bewail the condition of the reformed churches, who are come to a period in religion, and will go at present no further than the instruments of their reformation.—Luther and Calvin were great and shining lights in their times, yet they penetrated not into the whole counsel of God.—I beseech you, remember it,—'tis an article of your church covenant,— that you be ready to receive whatever truth shall be made known to you from the written word of God.[6]

Idle colonists bowling

In September of 1620, the Pilgrims set sail from Plymouth, England, in a ship named the *Mayflower*. After more than two months at sea, the *Mayflower* reached the American shore, but at a destination not specified by the original charter. The original charter had given the Pilgrim travelers the right to settle in the "northern parts of Virginia." The *Mayflower* had been drawn off course by stormy weather to a point that was north of the Virginia Company's jurisdiction, Provincetown Harbor in Massachusetts at the tip of Cape Cod. Need for a governing document forced the weary travelers to draft what has become known as the Mayflower Compact. The Compact was drafted and signed by forty-one adult males while all remained aboard ship. The Pilgrims did not disembark, but went on to Plymouth, where they landed in late December of that same year.

By the terms of the hastily constructed governing document, "the Pilgrims agreed to govern themselves until they could arrange for a charter of their own; they were never able to arrange for such a charter, and the Compact remained in force until their colony at Plymouth was absorbed in that of Massachusetts Bay in 1691."[7]

The preamble of the Mayflower Compact emphasizes religious themes and political loyalties that are reflected in later charters and state constitutions.

Sailing of the Pilgrims from Plymouth, England

Landing of the Pilgrims at Plymouth, Dec. 22, 1620

The Compact reads in part:

> In the name of God, Amen.
>
> We, whose names are underwritten, the loyal subjects of our dread Sovereign Lord King James, by the Grace of God of Great Britain, France, and Ireland, King, Defender of the Faith, etc.
>
> Having undertaken for the Glory of God and advancement of the Christian Faith, and Honour of our King and Country, a Voyage to plant the First Colony in the Northern Parts of Virginia; do by these presents solemnly and mutually in the presence of God and one another, Covenant and Combine ourselves together into a Civil Body Politic, for our better ordering and preservation and further-

William Bradford

> ance of other ends aforesaid; and by virtue hereof do enact, constitute and frame such just and equal Laws, Ordinances, Acts, Constitutions and Offices, from time to time, as shall be thought most [suitable] and convenient for the general good of the Colony, unto which we promise all due submission and obedience.

These early settlers to the New World brought with them an old faith, a faith rooted in "the name of God. . . . for the glory of God and advancement of the Christian faith." Those aboard the Mayflower were conscious of the fact that they were acting "in the presence of God" as they drafted what would later be called "the foundation stone of American liberty"[8] and the basis of representative government in the New World.

18

"[F]OR THE PROPAGATION AND ADVANCE OF THE GOSPEL ..."

PLYMOUTH PLANTATION

William Bradford followed John Carver as governor of Plymouth after Carver's death in 1621. In addition to his civil duties as governor, Bradford also wrote *Of Plymouth Plantation*, an eyewitness account of the history of the colony up through 1650. The manuscript had been passed down to several historians who used it as research in the publication of their own historical works. It was thought to be lost until it was discovered in 1855 in the library of the bishop of London. As Bradford's work demonstrates, the Pilgrims were motivated by evangelistic zeal:

[The colonists] cherished a great hope and inward zeal of laying good foundations, or at least of making some way towards it, for the propagation and advance of the gospel of the kingdom of Christ in the remote parts of the world, even though they should be but stepping stones to others in the performance of so great a work.[9]

Plymouth was first a religious society, second, an economic enterprise, and last, a political commonwealth governed by biblical standards. The religious convictions of the Pilgrims were early expressed in the drafting of the

The First Sunday at New Haven

Mayflower Compact and the settlement of the colony.

CONNECTICUT

New Haven was established by the Reverend John Davenport and Theophilus Eaton in 1638. It was at New Haven that the first general court convened and enacted a body of laws. "After a day of fasting and prayer, they rested their first frame of government on a simple plantation covenant, that 'all of them would be ordered by the rules which the Scriptures held forth to them.'"[10] Under the guidance of Davenport, who became the colony's pastor, and Eaton, who was annually elected its governor for twenty years until his death, the colony prospered and maintained its faithfulness to the Word of God.

A year after the meeting of the general court, the colonists desired a more perfect form of government. A committee consisting of Davenport, Eaton, and five others, who made up what was known as "the seven Pillars," enacted a civil polity where God's Word was "established as the only rule in public affairs. Thus New Haven made the Bible its statute-book, and the elect its freemen."[11]

After a period of war with the Indians, the settlers of the western colony resolved to perfect its political institutions and to form a body politic by voluntary association. It was on January 14, 1639, that the Fundamental Orders of Connecticut, often called the world's first written constitution, was adopted at Hartford.

It reads in part:

Forasmuch as it has pleased Almighty God by the wise disposition of His Divine Providence so to order and dispose of things that we the inhabitants and residents . . . ; and well knowing where a people are gathered together the Word of God requires that to maintain the peace and union of such a people there should be an orderly and decent government established according to God, to order and dispose of the affairs of all the people at all seasons as occasions shall require.

The founders further stated that one of the governing purposes of the document was "to maintain and preserve the liberty and purity of the Gospel of our Lord Jesus which we now profess, as also the discipline of the churches, which according to the truth of the said Gospel is now practiced among us."[12]

NEW ENGLAND CONFEDERATION

The New England Confederation, put into effect on May 19, 1643, established a union of like-minded civil bodies. They shared a common understanding of limited civil government and the need to advance the cause of the Gospel, a mission they described as "to advance the Kingdom of our Lord Jesus Christ and to enjoy the liberties of the Gospel in purity with peace."[13]

Civil rulers and judges were considered to be "ministers of God for the good of the people," to "have power to declare, publish, and establish, for the Plantations within their jurisdiction, the

New England Puritans going to Church

laws He hath made; and to make and repeal orders for smaller matters, not particularly determined in Scriptures, according to the more general rules of righteousness, and while they stand in force, to require execution of them."[14] These colonists showed their understanding of Scripture by acknowledging that while God sets forth specific laws in the Bible, He also expects those laws to be applied with wisdom as circumstances dictate.

CONCLUSION

From the First Charter of Virginia, granted by King James I in 1606 "to propagate the Christian religion," to the Pennsylvania Charter of Privileges granted to William Penn in 1701, where "all persons who . . . profess to believe in Jesus Christ, the Saviour of the World, shall be capable . . . to serve this Government in any capacity, both legislatively and executively," all the colonies were founded on the religious precepts of Christianity, with the Bible as their statute book.

William Penn

[1] "First Charter of Virginia" (April 10, 1606), *Documents of American History*, ed. Henry Steele Commager, 6th ed. (New York: Appleton-Century-Crofts, 1958), 8.

[2] Charles Lemuel Thompson, *The Religious Foundations of America: A Study in National Origins* (New York: Fleming H. Revell, 1917), 81-82.

[3] Thompson, *The Religious Foundations of America*, 83.

[4] Quoted in Paul S. Newman, *In God We Trust: America's Heritage of Faith* (Norwalk, CT: C.R. Gibson Co., 1974), 21.

[5] B. F. Morris, *The Christian Life and Character of the Civil Institutions of the United States* (Philadelphia, PA: George W. Childs, 1864), 94.

[6] George Bancroft, *History of the Colonization of the United States*, 10 vols. 4th ed. (Boston, MA: Charles C. Little and James Brown, 1837), 1:307.

[7] Mortimer J. Adler, ed., "The Mayflower Compact," *Annals of America: 1493-1754*, 18 vols. (Chicago, IL: Encyclopedia Britannica, 1968), 1:64.

[8] Frank R. Donovan, *The Mayflower Compact* (New York: Grosset & Dunlap, 1968), 12.

[9] William Bradford, *Bradford's History of the Plymouth Settlement*, 1608-1650, rendered into modern English by Harold Paget (Portland, OR: American Heritage Ministries, [1909] 1988), 21. For a history of Bradford's *Of Plymouth Plantation* and a modern complete text version with notes and an introduction, see Samuel Eliot Morison, ed., *Of Plymouth Plantation*, 1620–1647 (New York: Alfred A. Knopf, 1970).

[10] Bancroft, *History of the Colonization of the United States*, 1:403.

[11] Bancroft, *History of the Colonization of the United States*, 1:404.

[12] "Fundamental Orders of Connecticut" (January 14, 1639), *Documents*, 23.

[13] "The New England Confederation" (May 19, 1643), *Documents*, 26.

[14] *Code of New Haven* (1656), 567. Quoted in Isaac A. Cornelison, *The Relation of Religion to Civil Government in the United States of America: A State without a Church, But Not without a Religion* (New York: Knickerbocker Press, 1895), 59.

2

"THROUGH DIVINE GOODNESS"

CHRISTIANITY IN THE COLONIAL CONSTITUTIONS

Like the colonial charters that pre- ceded them, state constitutions expressed dependence on God for the maintenance of a moral civil order. These independent state govern- ments, with their representative offi- cials, created a constitutional system of government that has never been dupli- cated. The framers were wise enough to limit the power of the newly formed federal government by insisting that the states retain the major portion of their sovereignty. Powers not delegated to the national government through the Constitution remained with the states. This included religion, specifically the Christian religion and how it related to personal freedom and the maintenance of a just civil government. The state constitutions are a remarkable testimo- ny to the role that Christianity played in the formation of the American Republic.[1]

DELAWARE
"Liberty and Independence"
The Delaware Constitution established the Christian reli- gion, while not elevating "one religious sect" in the "State in pref- erence to another." A jurisdictional sep- aration between church and state was maintained by prohibiting a "clergyman or preacher of the gospel, of any denomination" from "holding any civil office" in the state "while they continue in the exercise of the pastoral function." Even so, Delaware did require its office holders to subscribe to certain religious beliefs:

> Every person who shall be chosen a member of either house, or appoint- ed to any office or place of trust . . . shall . . . also make and subscribe the following declaration, to wit:

> "I do profess faith in God the Father, and in Jesus Christ His only Son, and in the Holy Ghost, one God, blessed for evermore; and I do acknowledge the holy scriptures of the Old and New Testament to be given by divine inspiration."

Seal of Delaware

Revisions to the Delaware Constitution were made in 1792. The new Preamble declared, "Through divine goodness all men have, by nature, the rights of worshipping and serving their Creator according to the dictates of their consciences." The people of Delaware are exhorted "to assemble together for the public worship of the Author of the universe," although not through compulsion by the state. In addition, "piety and morality" are to be "promoted."

NEW JERSEY
"Liberty and Prosperity"

Seal of New Jersey

The earliest settlers in New Jersey were Christians who came from the eastern end of Long Island, New York. They settled at Elizabethtown, where the first colonial legislative assembly convened to transfer the chief features of New England laws to the statute book of New Jersey. The New Jersey Constitution of 1776 stipulated that "no person shall ever . . . be deprived of the inestimable privilege of worshipping Almighty God in a manner agreeable to the dictates of his own conscience." A citizen of New Jersey would not be compelled by state law "to attend any place of worship, contrary to his own faith and judgment." Neither would he be "obliged to pay tithes, taxes, or any other rates, for the purpose of building or repairing any church or churches, places of worship, or for the maintenance of any minister or ministry."

These religious liberty provisions did not disestablish Protestant Christianity. They merely stated that the civil government could not establish "any one religious sect . . . in preference to another." The constitution did give Protestants special constitutional privileges in that "no Protestant inhabitant of this Colony shall be denied the enjoyment of any civil right, merely on account of his religious principles; but that all persons, professing a belief in the faith of any Protestant sect . . . shall be capable of being elected into any office or profit or trust, or being a member of either branch of the Legislature."

The following instructions from the legislature of New Jersey to its delegates in Congress in 1777 exemplifies the Christian sentiments of the men who directed the civil and military concerns of the Revolution:

> We hope you will habitually bear in mind that the success of the great cause in which the United States are engaged depends upon the favor and blessing of Almighty God; and therefore you will neglect nothing which is competent to the Assembly of the States for promoting *piety* and *good morals* among the people at large.[2]

New Jersey's history of its Christian foundations goes back as far as 1683 with the drafting of the "Fundamental Constitution for the Province of East New Jersey." Religious liberty was upheld, and every civil magistrate was required to affirm this by law and swear a binding oath to Jesus Christ. Following this requirement we read:

24

"Nor by this article is it intended that any under the notion of liberty shall allow themselves to avow atheism, irreligiousness, or to practice cursing, swearing, drunkenness, profaneness, whoring, adultery, murdering, or any kind of violence. . . ."[3] Marriage was defined by "the law of God."[4]

GEORGIA

"Wisdom, Justice, Moderation"
General James Oglethorpe (1696-1785) conceived a plan to provide a refuge for persecuted Protestants of Europe. On June 9, 1732, he was granted a charter by George II to establish a new colony. Oglethorpe named his colony Georgia. He was motivated primarily from strong Christian principles, which are evident in his denouncement of slavery. In London, in 1734, he praised Georgia for its anti-slavery policy:

> Slavery, the misfortune, if not the dishonor, of other plantations, is absolutely proscribed. Let avarice defend it as it will, there is an honest reluctance in humanity against buying and selling, and regarding those of our species as our wealth and possessions. . . . The name of slavery is here unheard, and every inhabitant is free from unchosen masters and oppression. . . . Slavery is against the gospel as well as the fundamental law of England. We refused, as trustees, to make a law permitting such a horrid crime.[5]

Oglethorpe's words were not heeded. The "horrid crime" of slavery was soon introduced to Georgia. "In 1750 the

James Oglethorpe

law prohibiting slavery was repealed and Georgia became a slave-worked plantation colony like its neighbor, South Carolina."[6]

In keeping with the original charter which gave the colonists of Georgia "a liberty of conscience" to worship God, the 1777 constitution retains its essential religious character. Article VI states that "The representatives shall be chosen out of the residents in each county . . . and they shall be of the Protestant religion." Article LVI declares that "All persons whatever shall have the free exercise of their religion; provided it be not repugnant to the peace and safety of the State." The Preamble to the revised Georgia Constitution in 1945 stated: "To perpetuate the principles of free government, insure justice to all, preserve peace, promote the interest and happiness of the citizen, and transmit to posterity the enjoyment of liberty, we, the people of Georgia, relying upon the protection and guidance of Almighty God, do ordain and establish this Constitution."

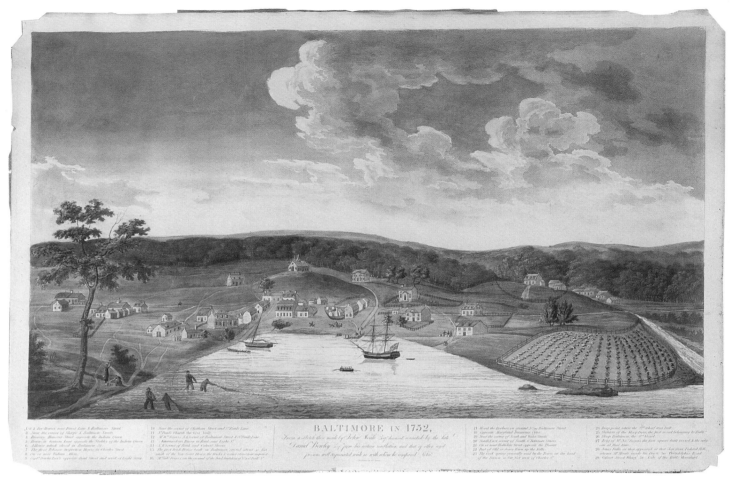

City of Baltimore

Seal of
Maryland

MARYLAND

*"With Favor Wilt Thou Compass
Us As With A Shield"*
(Psalm 5:12)[7]

While the other colonies
were settled by Protestant
Christians, Maryland was first
settled by English Catholics in
1634, under the direction of Cecilius
Calvert, Lord Baltimore (1606-1675).
Baltimore's proprietorship was often
challenged and was eventually lost when
Maryland became a royal colony in the
late seventeenth century.

It cannot be disputed, however, that
Maryland's civil government was dedi-
cated to defending orthodox Christianity.
Article XXXIII of its 1776 constitution
declares, "All persons, professing the
Christian religion, are equally entitled to
protection in their religious liberty;

Cecil Calvert and his grandson

26

wherefore no person ought by any law to be molested in his person or estate on account of his religious persuasion or profession, or for his religious practice; unless, under colour of religion, any man shall disturb the good order, peace and safety of the State."

Seal of Massachusetts

MASSACHUSETTS
"By the Sword We Seek Peace, but Peace Only Under Liberty"

Massachusetts has a long history of advancing and protecting the Christian religion. Its constitution of 1780 continues the state's Christian history by asserting that "It is the right as well as the duty of all men in society, publicly, and at stated seasons, to worship the SUPREME BEING, the great Creator and Preserver of the universe." After stating that the "governor shall be chosen annually," qualifications for holding office are next listed: "no person shall be eligible to this office, unless . . . he shall declare himself to be of the Christian religion." The following oath was also required: "I do declare, that I believe the Christian religion, and have firm persuasion of its truth."

NEW HAMPSHIRE
"Live Free or Die"

New Hampshire became a separate colony from Massachusetts in 1679. Because of its Puritan origins it shared the religious views of Massachusetts. The constitution of 1784 states:

Every individual has a natural and unalienable right to worship GOD according to the dictates of his own conscience, and reason; and no subject shall be hurt, molested, or restrained in his person, liberty or estate for worshipping GOD, in the manner and season most agreeable to the dictates of his own conscience, or for his religious profession, sentiments or persuasion; provided he doth not disturb the public peace, or disturb others, in their religious worship.

The constitution recognized that "morality and piety" are "rightly grounded on evangelical principles." State office holders—governor, senators, representatives, and members of Council—must be of the "protestant religion." New Hampshire's 1792 constitution, drafted after the ratification of the United States Constitution, retained all the religious liberties as well as all the religious restrictions of the 1784 constitution.

NORTH CAROLINA
"To Be Rather Than to Seem"

The French and Spanish were the first to explore the area of the Carolinas in the early sixteenth century. The English were the first to colonize the region. Sir Walter Raleigh led three expedition to the area. The first permanent colony was founded about 1653 near Albemarle Sound by settlers from Virginia. In 1711, Carolina was divided into North Carolina and South Carolina. North Carolina became a royal colony in 1729.

The 1776 Constitution of North Carolina upholds religious freedom. Article XIX reads, "All men have a natural and unalienable right to worship God according to the dictates of their own consciences." Article XXXII is more specifically Christian in specifying the following qualifications for public officers in the state: "No person who shall deny the being of God, or the truth of the Protestant religion, or the divine authority of the Old or New Testaments, or who shall hold religious principles incompatible with the freedom and safety of the State, shall be capable of holding any office or place of trust or profit in the civil department within this State." This provision remained in effect until 1876.

Sir Walter Raleigh

SOUTH CAROLINA
"Ready in Soul and Resource"

James Underwood, a professor at the University of South Carolina Law School, has stated that South Carolina's Constitution includes "provisions that are unconstitutional under the federal constitution."[8] These provisions, as of 1989, included the following:

Seal of South Carolina

- "No person shall be eligible to hold office of Governor who denies the existence of the Supreme Being."

- "No person who denies the existence of a Supreme Being shall hold any office under this constitution."

South Carolina's Constitution reflects principles set forth in the 1778 version. Article XXXVIII of the 1778 constitution assures that "all persons and religious societies who acknowledge that there is one God, and a future state of rewards and punishments, and that God is publicly to be worshipped, shall be freely tolerated." In addition, the "Christian Protestant religion shall be deemed, and is hereby constituted and declared to be, the established religion of this State." While religious requirements were mandated by law for all who held political office, "No person shall, by law, be obliged to pay towards the maintenance and support of a religious worship that he does not freely join in, or has not voluntarily engaged in support."

PENNSYLVANIA

"Virtue, Liberty, and Independence"

Pennsylvania was founded by William Penn, a Quaker who had once been imprisoned for blasphemy. In his 1682 "Charter of Liberties," Penn cited the biblical origin of civil government, and maintained, citing 1 Timothy 1:9-10, that the law of God was made for the unrighteous. He went on to cite Romans 13:1-5: "This settles the divine right of government beyond exception, and that for two ends. First, to terrify evil doers; secondly, to cherish those that do well."[9]

A 1705-06 act of the Pennsylvania legislature to regulate the number of members of the assembly required that to serve as a civil magistrate, a person had to "also profess to believe in Jesus Christ, the saviour of the world" and take the following oath: "I profess faith in God the Father and in Jesus Christ his eternal son, the true God, and in the Holy Spirit, one God blessed for evermore; and do acknowledge the Holy Scriptures of the Old and New Testament to be given by divine inspiration."[10]

The Pennsylvania Constitution of 1776 declared that the legislature shall consist of "persons most noted for wisdom and virtue," and that every member should subscribe to the following:

> I do believe in one God, the Creator and Governor of the universe, the Rewarder of the good and the Punisher of the wicked; and I acknowledge the Scriptures of the Old and New Testaments to be given by Divine inspiration.

The 1790 constitution reaffirms the liberties established in 1776 and goes on to affirm, "That no person, who acknowledges the being of God, and a future state of rewards and punishments, shall, on account of his religious sentiments, be disqualified to hold any office or place of trust or profit under this commonwealth."

William Penn

ALL OF THE COLONIAL CONSTITUTIONS ACKNOWLEDGED THAT GOD HAD A HAND IN THEIR FOUNDING AND DEVELOPMENT.

CONCLUSION

All of the colonial constitutions acknowledged that God had a hand in their founding and development. "Even in the fundamental law of the Province of Rhode Island," best known for the religious dissension of its founder Roger Williams, "Christian purpose is expressly stated and a particular form of Christianity (Protestantism) was required as a qualification for office."[11]

Seal of Rhode Island

[1]The material in this chapter can be found in a number of sources: Francis Newton Thorpe, *The Federal and State Constitutions, Colonial Charters, and Other Organic Laws of the States, Territories, and Colonies,* 7 vols. (Washington, D.C.: 1909) and W. Keith Kavenaugh, ed., *Foundations of Colonial America: A Documentary History,* 3 vols. (New York: Chelsea House, 1973). Edwin S. Gaustad's *Neither King Nor Prelate: Religion and the New Nation, 1776–1826* (Grand Rapids, MI: Eerdmans, 1993) includes similar and more accessible information but in an abbreviated form.

[2]Cited in Morris, *Christian Life and Character of the Civil Institutions of the United States,* 235.

[3]"Fundamental Constitution for the Province of East New Jersey, 1683," in W. Keith Kavenaugh, ed., *Foundations of Colonial America,* 3 vols. (New York: Chelsea House, 1973), 2:1107.

[4]"Fundamental Constitution for the Province of East New Jersey, 1683," in Kavenaugh, *Foundations of Colonial America,* 2:1108.

[5]Jesse T. Peck, *The History of the Great Republic, Considered from a Christian Stand-Point* (New York: Broughton and Wyman, 1868), 80.

[6]Irwin Unger, *Instant American History: Through the Civil War and Reconstruction* (New York: Fawcett Columbine, 1994), 34.

[7]Also appearing on Maryland's seal is the motto "Strong Deeds, Gentle Words."

[8]Reported by Tom Strong, "S.C. Constitution labeled archaic," *The Sun News* (Myrtle Beach, South Carolina) (July 9, 1989), 3D.

[9]"Charter of Liberties and Frame of Government of Pennsylvania, April 25-May 5, 1682," in Kavenaugh, *Foundations of Colonial America,* 2:1134.

[10]"Act to Ascertain the Number of Members of Assembly and to Regulate the Election, 1705-06," in Kavenaugh, *Foundations of Colonial America,* 2:1169.

[11]Isaac A. Cornelison, *The Relation of Religion to Civil Government in the United States of America: A State Without a Church, But Not Without a Religion* (New York: G.P Putnam's Sons, 1895), 85.

3

"IN THE YEAR OF OUR LORD"

CHRISTIANITY AND THE CONSTITUTION

Alexander Hamilton

A story has been told about a chance meeting between a minister and Alexander Hamilton after the Philadelphia Convention had adjourned.[1] The minister asked Hamilton why "the Constitution has no recognition of God or the Christian religion." Hamilton is reported to have said, "We forgot it."[2] Many now ask how it is possible that men from states whose constitutions were not shy about acknowledging God, could leave out any mention of Him in the Federal Constitution. Certainly, biblical principles of limited and representative government, a sound monetary policy, the establishment of justice, the maintenance of liberty, and the preservation of peace are biblical principles that ripple through the document.[3] But is the Constitution without any mention of God or the Christian religion? Only a study of history will tell us.

A POLITICAL DOCUMENT

As we have seen, the state constitutions were explicitly Christian in their design. The Federal Constitution, as a creation of the states, did not nullify the states' rights to govern their religious affairs. The absence of direct references to God and the Christian religion in the Constitution, as compared to the state constitutions, is due in part from an understanding that it was drafted for

Independence Hall

31

Dr. Philip Schaff

a very limited civil objective. Since the thirteen colonies/states had their own constitutions, governors, and representatives, the newly created national government would only do what the several states could not do individually. Powers not delegated to the national government remained with the states. Church historian Philip Schaff offers the following defense for the absence of references to Providence, the Creator, nature and nature's God, and the Supreme Being in terms of the document's political purpose:

> The absence of the names of God and Christ, in a purely political and legal document, no more proves denial or irreverence than the absence of those names in a mathematical treatise, or the statutes of a bank or railroad corporation. The title "Holiness" does not make the Pope of Rome any holier than he is. . . . The book of Esther and the Song of Solomon are undoubtedly productions of devout worshippers of Jehovah; and yet the name of God does not occur once in them.[4]

The argument is that theology did not draw the delegates to Philadelphia in 1787. These issues had already been settled at the state level. Instead, the delegates came to debate and construct the best form of civil government at the national level.

A CAMPAIGN TO DECHRISTIANIZE A NATION

There were two revolutions at the end of the eighteenth century, two new constitutions drafted, two nations formed, and two different reactions to the Christian religion. France was caught up in revolutionary fever in 1791, not with a foreign power but with itself. The French revolutionaries were self-conscious about their efforts to turn France into a secular state, devoid of any remnant of religion. Throughout

The Effects of the Anti-Christian French Revolution

the nation a "campaign to dechristianize France spread like wildfire."[5] The dechristianization of the French Republic meant the crowning of a substitute civil religion. The leaders of the Paris Commune demanded that the former metropolitan church of Notre Dame be reconsecrated as a "Temple of Reason." On November 10, 1793, a civic festival was held in the new temple, its façade bearing the words "To Philosophy." In Paris, the goddess Reason "was personified by an actress, Demoiselle Candeille, carried shoulder-high into the cathedral by men dressed in Roman costumes."[6] The Commune ordered that all churches be closed and converted into poor houses and schools. "Church bells were melted down and used to cast cannons."[7]

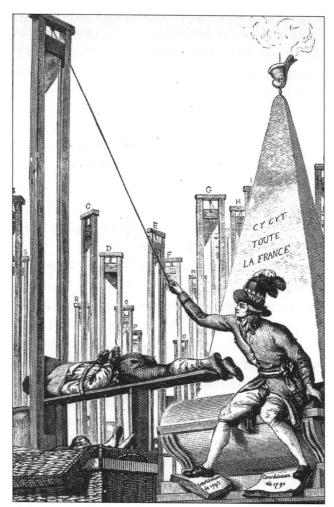
Robespierre guillotining the executioner

Blatant infidelity precipitated that storm of pitiless fury. The National Assembly passed a resolution deliberately declaring "There is no God;" vacated the throne of Deity by simple resolution, abolished the Sabbath, unfrocked her ministers of religion, turned temples of spiritual worship into places of secular business, and enthroned a vile woman as the Goddess of Reason.[8]

The French Revolution replaced the God of Revelation with the Goddess of Reason, with disastrous results. Blood literally flowed in the streets as day after day "enemies of the republic" met their death under the sharp blade of Madame Guillotine. "France, in its terrific revolution, saw the violent culmination of theoretical and practical infidelity."[9]

The French calendar was also changed to reflect the new anti-Christian spirit of the revolution. "The Convention voted on 5 October 1793 to abolish the Christian calendar and introduce a republican calendar."[10] The founding of the Republic on September 22, 1792, was the beginning of the new era and a new "Year One." Instead of the birth of Jesus Christ being the focal point of history, the founding day of the new French Republic would define how time would be kept. While the year still had twelve months, all were made thirty days long with the remaining days scattered throughout the year and celebrated as festival days. The seven-day week was replaced with a week of ten

THE CONSTITUTION ITSELF STATES THAT THE DRAFTING TOOK PLACE "IN THE YEAR OF OUR LORD ..."

days with the result that Sunday as a day of rest and Christian worship was eliminated.[11]

The French Republic went beyond a new calendar by changing place names that had "reference to a Christian past." In addition, "children were named after republican heroes such as Brutus and Cato, and observance of the new Revolutionary calendar, which abolished Sunday and Christian Feast days, was enforced.[12]

CHRISTIAN CONTINUITY

When compared to what the French did, the United States Constitution establishes continuity with the nation's Christian past by linking it with the Christian calendar. Article 1, section 7 of our Constitution exempts *Sunday* as a day to be counted within which the president may veto legislation. If the framers had wanted to strip every vestige of religion from the Constitution,

why include a reference to an obvious religious observance? Sunday observance remained under constitutional protection at the federal and state levels for some time in the United States. As Supreme Court Justice David Brewer observed, the recognition of Sunday as a day of worship and rest is "a day peculiar to [the Christian] faith, and known to no other."[13]

The Constitution itself states that the drafting took place "in the year of our Lord one thousand seven hundred and eighty-seven." This might seem insignificant to some, but when compared to what the French did in creating a new "Year One," it takes on special meaning. The constitutional framers could have taken the direction of the French Revolutionaries and created a "new order of the ages" based on a new calendar if they had wanted to make a complete break with the Christian past. They did not.

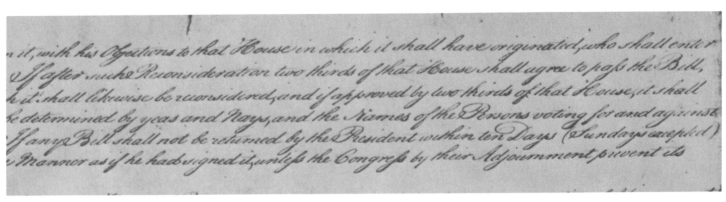

Article 1, Section 7, of the Constitution

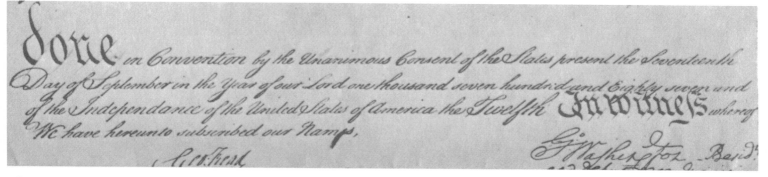

from the Constitution: "DONE . . . in the year of our Lord"

RELIGIOUS DISCORD AND STATES RIGHTS

One theory to explain why the Constitution addresses religion only in an indirect way is because there were different Christian denominations represented at the constitutional convention in Philadelphia: Congregationalist, Episcopalian, Dutch Reformed, Presbyterian, Quaker, Lutheran, Roman Catholic, and Methodist.[14] "James Madison tells us there was 'discord of religious opinions within the convention,' which undoubtedly kept theological controversy off the floor."[15] Some maintain that the proliferation of religious opinions among the delegates steered the convention away from including specific religious language in the Constitution.

A variation of Madison's explanation is that the representatives wanted to guard the states from federal intrusion, preserving the authority of the states to establish their own religious parameters. Since the religious issue was already settled at the state level, there was no need for the federal government to meddle in an area in which the national government would have no jurisdiction. The prohibition of a religious test in Article VI, section 3 "as a qualification to any office or public trust under the United States" applied only to *national* office holders: congressmen, senators, the president, and Supreme Court Justices. States were free to apply their own test and oath, which they did. Schaff maintained that the article's inclusion secured "the freedom and independence of the State from ecclesiastical domination and interference."[16]

The First Amendment as well as the "no religious test" provision "are expressly made to apply to the general government alone. They do not apply to the States. It may have been the intent in framing the Constitution to assign the matter of religion to the domain of the States, rather than to accomplish an elimination of all religious character from our civil institutions."[17] In his *Commentary on the Constitution of the United States*, Supreme Court Justice Joseph Story

Joseph Story

(1779-1845) wrote, "Thus, the whole power over the subject of religion was left exclusively to the State governments, to be acted on according to their own sense of justice, and the State Constitutions."[18]

Story's *Commentary* clearly shows that the First Amendment was designed to prohibit the federal establishment of a national Church or the official preference of a particular Christian sect over all others. The First Amendment, according to Story, was not designed to disestablish the Christian religion at the state level, but only to insure that no single Christian sect (denomination) would be established in terms of constitutional preference:

> Probably, at the time of the adoption of the Constitution, and of the . . . [First Amendment], the general, if not the universal, sentiment in America was, that Christianity ought to receive encouragement from the State, so far as such encouragement was not incompatible with the private rights of conscience, and the freedom of religious worship. An attempt to level all religions, and to make it a matter of state policy to hold all in utter indifference, would have created universal disapprobation, if not universal indignation.[19]

While the national government received new powers as a result of the ratification of the Constitution, denying the states jurisdiction over religious issues was not one of them. The Tenth Amendment supports this view: "The powers, not delegated to the United States by the Constitution, nor prohibited by it to the States, are reserved to the States, respectively, or to the people." In the Circuit Court of Tennessee, August 1, 1891, the Court said, "As a matter of fact they (the founders of our government) left the States the most absolute power on the subject, any of them might, if they chose, establish a creed and a church and maintain them."[20]

CHRISTIANITY ASSUMED

Another argument put forth to explain the Constitution's lack of explicit religious language "is that the Christian premises of the American Constitution and the people's reliance on the Christian deity were assumed by the framers, and thus explicit reference was unnecessary. 'The Bible,' argued Robert Baird, the trailblazing student of religion in America, 'does not begin with an argument to prove the existence of God, but assumes the fact, as one [of] the truth[s] of which it needs no attempt to establish.'"[21] Having said this, even Baird had to acknowledge his regret at the absence of "something more explicit on the subject. . . . Sure I am that, had the excellent men who framed the Constitution foreseen the inferences that have been drawn from the omission, they would have recognized, in a proper formula, the existence of God, and the truth and the importance of the Christian religion."[22] The belief was that Christianity was so much a cornerstone of American thought and law that there was no need to make it an official constitutional declaration. Cornelison expressed the prevailing Protestant view of the time that "the government of these United States was necessarily, rightfully, and lawfully Christian."[23]

CONCLUSION

If the constitutional framers could get a glimpse of America today, would they have rethought their decision only to make passing reference to the lordship of Jesus Christ in the body of the Constitution? Would they have been more specific in their mention of God and the need for the nation's reliance on Him in light of the secularizing spirit that seems to have America in its grip?

Signing of the U.S. Constitution

We will never know. But when all the testimony is in, it is an undeniable truth that Christianity served as the foundation for the political edifice we know as America. In 1982, Congress declared 1983 to be the "Year of the Bible."

In that official pronouncement it is stated that "biblical teachings inspired concepts of civil government that are contained in our Declaration of Independence and the Constitution."[24]

[1]No one knows for sure the identity of the questioner or whether the encounter actually took place. B.F. Morris identifies him as the Rev. Dr. Miller, a distinguished professor at Princeton College (*The Christian Life and Character of the Civil Institutions of the United States* [Philadelphia, PA: George W. Childs, 1864], 248). Isaac A. Cornelison identifies him as Rev. Dr. John Rogers, a chaplain of the War of Independence and Presbyterian minister (*The Relation of Religion to Civil Government in the United States of America: A State Without a Church, But Not Without a Religion* [New York: G.P Putnam's Sons, 1895], 204).

[2]George Duffield, Jr., "The God of Our Fathers, An Historical Sermon," Preached in the Coates' Street Presbyterian Church, Philadelphia, on Fast Day, January 4, 1861 (Philadelphia, PA: T.B. Pugh, 1861), 15. See Morris, *Christian Life and Character*, 248. Further references can be found in Daniel L. Dreisbach, "God and the Constitution: Reflections on Selected Nineteenth Century Commentaries on References to the Deity and the Christian Religion in the States Constitution," 22, note 77. This paper is unpublished.

[3]Gary DeMar, *God and Government: A Biblical and Historical Study* (Powder Springs, GA: American Vision, 1990), 141–167 and Archie P. Jones, *Christian Principles in the Constitution and the Bill of Rights* (Marlborough, NH: Plymouth Rock Foundation, 1994).

[4]Philip Schaff, *Church and State in the United States or The American Idea of Religious Liberty And Its Practical Effects* (New York: Charles Scribner's Sons, 1889), 40.

[5]Walter Grab, *The French Revolution: The Beginning of Modern Democracy* (London: Bracken Books, 1989), 165.

[6]Francis A. Schaeffer, *How Should We Then Live?* (1976) in *The Complete Works of Francis A. Schaeffer: A Christian Worldview*, 5 vols. (Wheaton, IL: Crossway Books, 1984), 5:149.

[7]Grab, *The French Revolution*, 166.

[8]Charles B. Galloway, *Christianity and the American Commonwealth; or, The Influence of Christianity in Making This Nation* (Nashville, TN: Publishing House Methodist Episcopal Church, 1898), 25.

[9]Jesse T. Peck, *The History of the Great Republic Considered from a Christian Stand-Point* (New York: Broughton and Wyman, 1868), 321.

[10]Grab, *The French Revolution*, 165. Also see "Marking Time: Different Ways to Count the Changing Seasons," *Did You Know? New Insight into the World that is Full of Astonishing Stories and Astounding Facts* (London: *Reader's Digest*, 1990), 267.

[11]Grab, *The French Revolution*, 165.

[12]Richard Cobb, gen. ed., *Voices of the French Revolution* (Topsfield, MA: Salem House Publishers, 1988), 202. Also see Simon Schama, *Citizens: A Chronicle of the French Revolution* (New York: Alfred A. Knopf, 1989), 771-80.

[13]David J. Brewer, *The United States: A Christian Nation* (Philadelphia, PA: 1905), 26.

[14]M.E. Bradford, *A Worthy Company: The Dramatic Story of the Men Who Founded Our Country* (Wheaton, IL: Crossway Books, [1982] 1988).

[15]R. Kemp Morton, *God in the Constitution* (Nashville, TN: Cokesbury Press, 1933), 71.

[16]Schaff, *Church and State in the United States*, 21.

[17]Cornelison, *Relation of Religion to Civil Government in the United States of America*, 94.

[18]Joseph Story, *Commentary on the Constitution of the United States* (Boston, MA: Hilliard, Gray, and Co., 1833), 702-3. Story served as a justice of the United States Supreme Court from 1811 to 1845.

[19]Joseph Story, *A Familiar Exposition of the Constitution of the United States* (Lake Bluff, IL: Regnery Gateway, [1859] 1986), 316.

[20]*The Federal Reporter*, vol. 46, 912. Quoted in Cornelison, *Relation of Religion to Civil Government in the United States of America*, 95.

[21]Dreisbach, "God and the Constitution," 28.

[22]Robert Baird, *Religion in America; or, an Account of the Origin, Progress, Relation to the State, and Present Condition of the Evangelical Churches in the United States. With Notices of the Unevangelical Denominations* (New York: Harper & Brothers, 1844), 119. Quoted in Dreisbach, "God and the Constitution," 29.

[23]Cornelison, *The Relation of Religion to Civil Government in the United States of America*, 341.

[24]Public Law No. 97-280, 96 Stat. 1211 (October 4, 1982).

4

"TO LAY CHRIST AT THE BOTTOM"

CHRISTIANITY IN THE COLLEGES

"One of the most useful tools in the quest for power is the educational system."[1] The implication of this statement is obvious: Whoever controls the schools will set the goals for the nation, establish its religious values, and ultimately control the future. From Sparta and Athens to Geneva and Harvard, education has been the primary means of cultural transformation.

Christian educators learned how important education was for advancing Christian civilization. The Reformation of the sixteenth century stressed the reclamation of all of life, with education as an essential transforming force. Martin Luther in Germany (1483-1546) and John Calvin (1509-1564) in Geneva, Switzerland, did much to advance education as they worked to apply the Bible to every area of life. For these principal reformers, the outgrowth of the Gospel included the redemption of all of life, not just the salvation of the soul.

The Academy of Geneva, founded by John Calvin in 1559, attracted students from all over Europe eager for an education that applied the Bible to

John Calvin

all of life. The effects of the training at Geneva were far reaching: "It was not only the future of Geneva but that of other regions as well that was affected by the rise of the Geneva schools. The men who were to lead the advance of the Reformed Church in many lands were trained in Geneva classrooms, preached Geneva doctrines, and sang the Psalms to Geneva tunes."[2]

"EDUCATION WITHOUT THE BIBLE IS USELESS" —NOAH WEBSTER

Samuel Blumenfeld writes of the impact that Christian education had on the advancing reformation:

> The Bible was to be the moral and spiritual authority in every man's life, and therefore an intimate knowledge of it was imperative if a new Protestant social order were to take root.[3]

College of William and Mary

In our own nation, one of the first acts accomplished in the New World was the establishment of schools and colleges. The Virginia colony was the first to charter a college at Henrico in 1619, nineteen years before Harvard and seventy-four years before the College of William and Mary. Like all the colonial colleges, Henricus College was designed around the precepts of the Christian faith, "for the training and bringing up of infidels' children to the true knowledge of God and under-

standing of righteousness."[4] The New England colonial colleges were designed to further the Gospel of Christ in all disciplines. The founders of these early educational institutions understood the relationship between a sound education based upon biblical absolutes and the future of the nation. Putting the Bible in the hands of the people was an essential first step toward religious and political freedom. "From the very beginnings, the expressed purpose of colonial education had been to preserve society against barbarism, and, so far as possible, against sin. The inculcation of a saving truth was primarily the responsibility of the churches, but schools were necessary to protect the written means of revelation."[5] This is why Noah Webster, educator and compiler of the *1828 An American Dictionary of the English Language*, expressed the convictions of the earliest founders when he maintained that "Education without the Bible is useless."

Noah Webster

40

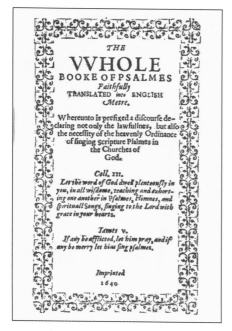

The Whole Book of Psalmes *title page*

A COLONIAL CURRICULUM

A young colonist's education in New England was provided by a curriculum that consisted of three books in addition to the Bible: the *Hornbook*, the *New England Primer*, and the *Bay Psalm Book*. The *Hornbook* consisted of a single piece of parchment, covered with a transparent substance attached to a paddle-shaped piece of wood. The alphabet, the Lord's Prayer, and religious doctrines were written or printed on the parchment.

In 1690, the first edition of the *New England Primer* appeared. By 1700, the Primer had replaced the *Hornbook* in a number of places. The *Primer* expanded the religious themes by including the names of the Old and New Testament books, the Lord's Prayer, "An Alphabet of Lessons for Youth," the Apostles' Creed, the Ten Commandments, the Westminster Assembly Shorter Catechism, and John Cotton's "Spiritual Milk for American Babes."

The *Primer*, developed by Benjamin Harris, included an ingenious way to learn the alphabet while mastering basic biblical truths and lessons about life.

A In **A**dam's Fall,
We sinned all

B Thy Life to mend,
This **B**ook attend

C The **C**at doth play,
And after slay

The *Primer* was later enlarged in 1777. Additional biblical material was added. The rhyming alphabet was updated and made more Bible-centered. For example, in the 1777 edition the letter **C** reads "Christ Crucified, For Sinners Died."

A typical Hornbook

Page from The Primer

HIGHER EDUCATION IN COLONIAL AMERICA

When Duke University was established in 1924, its founding bylaws stated: "The aims of Duke University are to assert a faith in the eternal union of knowledge and religion set forth in the teachings and character of Jesus Christ, the Son of God."[6] A study of colonial colleges will show that the character of Duke's founding was nearly identical to those colleges started in the seventeenth century. As the following chart demonstrates, with the exception of the University of Pennsylvania (1755), all of the colonial schools began as distinctly Christian institutions. Unfortunately, Duke and its educational predecessors no longer hold to their original denominational affiliations or their religious affirmations.

DATE	COLLEGE	COLONY	AFFILIATION
1636	Harvard	Massachusetts	Puritan
1693	William and Mary	Virginia	Anglican
1701	Yale	Connecticut	Congregational
1746	Princeton	New Jersey	Presbyterian
1754	King's College (Columbia)	New York	Anglican
1764	Brown	Rhode Island	Baptist
1766	Rutgers	New Jersey	Dutch Reformed
1769	Dartmouth	New Hampshire	Congregational

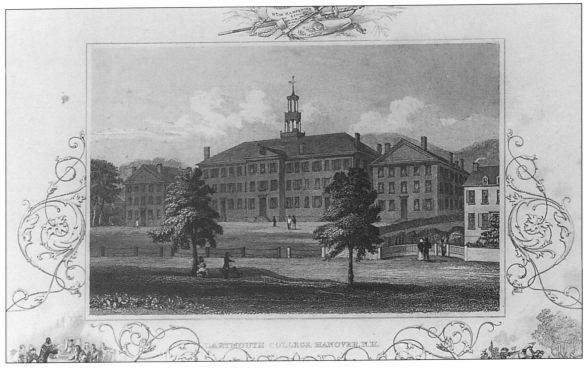

Dartmouth College

John Eliot preaching to the Indians

COLONIAL COLLEGES AND RELIGIOUS AFFILIATION

While most of the earliest colleges were established to train men for the Gospel ministry, the curriculum was much more comprehensive than the study of divinity. "Regardless of the vocation for which a student was preparing, the colonial college sought to provide for him an education that was distinctly Christian."[7] The curriculum of Harvard, for example, emphasized the study of biblical languages, logic, divinity (theology), and skills in communication (public speaking and rhetoric). The study of Latin linked students to classical studies and the writings of the church fathers going back to the first century. Ministers were often the most educated people in the colonies.

HARVARD (MASSACHUSETTS)

John Eliot (1604-1690), who is known as the "Apostle to the Indians," first proposed a college for Massachusetts Bay in 1633. Eliot's desires were realized three years later in the founding of Harvard College. (Harvard was named after John Harvard, who donated his library to the fledgling institution, and thus secured for himself a name in history.)

A Prospect of the Colledges in Cambridge in New England

The founders of Harvard wanted the Christian legacy they brought with them from England to continue. One of the best ways to accomplish this was to train men for the Gospel ministry. The following history, taken from *New England's First Fruits* (1643), explains what led to the founding of Harvard College.

> After God had carried us safe to *New England* and we had built our houses, provided necessities for our livelihood, raised convenient places for God's worship, and settled the Civil Government: One of the next things we longed for and looked after was to advance *Learning* and perpetuate it to posterity; dreading to leave an illiterate ministry to the churches, when our present Ministers shall lie in the Dust.[8]

Fifty-two percent of the seventeenth-century Harvard graduates became ministers.[9] The Puritans "did not distinguish sharply between secular and theological learning; and they believed that the collegiate education proper for a minister should be the same as for an educated layman. They expected that the early colleges would produce not only ministers but Christian gentlemen who would be civic leaders."[10]

44

"LET EVERY STUDENT BE PLAINLY INSTRUCTED ... THE MAIN END OF HIS LIFE AND STUDIES IS, TO KNOW GOD AND JESUS CHRIST..."

—HARVARD'S 1646 "RULES AND PRECEPTS"

While entry to Harvard required a thorough knowledge of Greek and Latin, a commitment to Jesus Christ and a belief that the Bible was the foundation for truth were even more essential. Harvard's "Rules and Precepts," adopted in 1646, included the following requirements:

2. Let every student be plainly instructed, and earnestly pressed to consider well, the main end of his life and studies is, to know God and Jesus Christ which is eternal life (John 17:3) and therefore lay Christ at the bottom, as the only foundation of all sound knowledge and learning.

And seeing the Lord only giveth wisdom, Let every one seriously set himself by prayer in secret to seek it of him, Proverbs 2:3.

3. Every one shall so exercise himself in reading the Scriptures twice a day, that he shall be ready to give such an account of his proficiency therein, both in *Theoretical* observations of the language, and *Logic*, and in *Practical* and spiritual truths, as his Tutor shall require, according to his ability; seeing *the entrance of the word giveth light, it giveth understanding to the simple,* Psalm 119:130.

An early motto of Harvard was *Veritas Christo et Ecclesiae* ("Truth for Christ and the Church"). "Religion was so much a part of everyday learning in the early days of Harvard that for nearly two centuries no one thought of setting up a separate Divinity School. In the college, students gathered daily for prayer and readings from the Scripture. Hebrew as well as Greek were required subjects, because an educated person was expected to be able to read the Bible in the original tongues."[11] Harvard's current motto has been reduced simply to *Veritas.*

YALE (CONNECTICUT)

By the eighteenth century, a growing number of New England colonists believed that Harvard had drifted from its original course. Increase Mather, president of Harvard from 1685 to 1701, and his son, Cotton Mather, had hoped they could prevent Harvard's change in course. They failed.

Yale College

Soon a new institution of learning was founded. Yale College was established in 1701 in Connecticut. "The founders of Yale required the 'Westminster Confession to be diligently read in the Latin Tongue and well studied by all the Scholars,' 'for the upholding of the Christian protestant Religion by a succession of Learned and Orthodox men.' The State of Connecticut in the Yale Charter of 1701 asserted its desire to support 'so necessary and Religious an undertaking.'"[12]

The founders of Yale yearned to return to the Christian foundation first laid at Harvard: "Yale in the early 1700s stated as its primary goal that 'every student shall consider the main end of his study to wit to know God in Jesus Christ and answerably to lead a Godly, sober life.'"[13] Yale demanded the same rigorous academic concentration as Harvard as well as a religious commitment to the cause of Christ and His Word: "All scholars shall live religious, godly, and blameless lives according to the rules of God's Word, diligently reading the Holy Scriptures, the fountain of light and truth; and constantly attend upon all the duties of religion, both in public and secret."[14] The Yale Charter of 1745 made it clear that the College, "Which has received the favourable benefactions of many liberal [generous] and piously disposed persons, and under the blessing of Almighty God has trained up many worthy persons for the service of God in the state as well as in the church."[15]

KING'S COLLEGE (NEW YORK)

An advertisement appeared in the *New York Mercury* on June 3, 1754, announcing the opening of King's College, known today as Columbia University. The advertisement had been placed by Samuel Johnson (1696-1772), a graduate of Yale. In 1754 the theologian and philosopher accepted an invitation to become the first president of King's College, an office he held until 1763. Similar to the guidelines demanded by Harvard and Yale, King's College required a knowledge of Latin and Greek. Although the college was affiliated with the Anglican Church, the advertisement assured students and parents that "there is no intention to impose on the scholars the peculiar tenets of any particular sect of Christians, but to inculcate upon their tender minds the great principles of Christianity and morality in which true Christians of each denomination are generally agreed."[16] The advertisement went on to state:

> The chief thing that is aimed at in this college is to teach and engage the children to know God in Jesus Christ and to love and serve Him in all sobriety, godliness, and righteousness of life, with perfect heart and a willing mind, and to train them up in all virtuous habits and all such useful knowledge as may render them creditable to their families and friends, ornaments to their country, and useful to the public weal in their generations.[17]

King's College Shield

Shield of Columbia University

The original shield of King's College was adopted in 1755. The college's commitment to a biblical worldview is evident in the shield's figures and inscriptions. Over the head of the seated woman is the (Hebrew) Tetragrammaton, YHVH (Jehovah); the Latin motto around her head means "In Thy light we see light" (Psalm 36:9); the Hebrew phrase on the ribbon is Uri El ("God is my light"), an allusion to Psalm 27:1; and at the feet of the woman is the New Testament passage commanding Christians to desire the pure milk of God's Word (1 Peter 2:1-2).[18] Columbia long ago adopted a new seal. The only line remaining from the original shield is the Latin phrase "In Thy light we see light" without any reference to its biblical source.

WILLIAM AND MARY (VIRGINIA)

In 1662, the Assembly of Virginia passed an act to make permanent provision for the establishment of a college. The preamble of the act recites "that the want of able and faithful ministers in this country deprives us of those great blessings and mercies that always attend upon the service of God"; and the act itself declares "that for the advancement of learning, education of youth, supply of the ministry, and promotion of piety, there be land taken up and purchased for a college and free school, and that with all convenient speed there be buildings erected upon it for the entertainment of students and scholars."[19]

Although an act had passed for the establishment of a college, the College of William and Mary was not actually founded until 1693. But like nearly all the colonial schools, William and Mary began with an evangelical purpose. The school would supply the church of Virginia "with a Seminary of Ministers" that the "Christian Faith may be propagated amongst the Western Indians, to the Glory of Almighty God."[20] These and other evangelical goals were reiterated in 1727.

CONCLUSION

The establishment of schools in the colonies was a way of maintaining and advancing the Christian faith. Education, therefore, was a religious exercise: "The schools were intended to form Christian men, Christian citizens, and Christian ministers, not as a by-product, but directly. They were instruments of the Church, which was, at least in the beginning, virtually coterminous with the community. Education was an enterprise undertaken primarily in the interests of religion, with religion, of course, defined in terms of the Calvinist orthodoxy then dominant in New England."[21]

In time, however, a philosophical shift took place. Colleges and universities in the nineteenth century were built by wealthy entrepreneurs for decidedly secular purposes. "Ezra Cornell (telegraph, banking), Johns Hopkins (banking, railroads), Cornelius Vanderbilt (steamships, railroads), Leland Stanford (railroads), James Duke (tobacco), and James D. Rockefeller (oil) were only a few of the prominent businessmen who poured vast sums into the creation of modern universities."[22] Some institu-

tions were more secular than others. For example, Andrew Dickson White, the founding president of Cornell University, promised that he would use the institution to "afford asylum for Science—where truth shall be sought for truth's sake, where it shall not be the main purpose of the Faculty to stretch or cut sciences exactly to fit 'Revealed Religion.'"[23]

America's institutions of higher learning have come a long way—from Harvard's declaration that the main end of man's life is to "know God and Jesus Christ which is eternal life (John 17:3)" to viewing Darwinian evolution as "a scientifically credible theory of random and purposeless change."[24]

[1]Herbert Schlossberg, *Idols for Destruction: Christian Faith and Its Confrontation with American Society* (Wheaton, IL: Crossway Books, [1983] 1993), 209.

[2]John T. McNeill, *The History and Character of Calvinism* (New York: Oxford University Press, 1954), 196.

[3]Samuel L. Blumenfeld, *Is Public Education Necessary?* (Old Greenwich, CT: Devin-Adair, 1981), 10.

[4]"Funds for a College at Henrico, Virginia (1619)," in Sol Cohen, ed., *Education in the United States: A Documentary History*, 5 vols. (New York: Random House, 1974), 1:336.

[5]Henry F. May, *The Enlightenment in America* (New York: Oxford University Press, 1976), 32-33.

[6]Quoted in George M. Marsden, *The Soul of the American University: From Protestant Establishment to Established Nonbelief* (New York: Oxford University Press, 1994), 322.

[7]William C. Ringenberg, *The Christian College: A History of Protestant Higher Education in America* (Grand Rapids, MI: Eerdmans, 1984), 38.

[8]Reprinted in Richard Hofstadter and Wilson Smith, eds., *American Higher Education: A Documentary History* (Chicago, IL: University of Chicago Press, 1961), 1:9.

[9]Marsden, *Soul of the American University*, 41.

[10]Hofstadter and Smith, "From the Beginnings to the Great Awakening," *American Higher Education*, 1:1.

[11]Ari L. Goldman, *The Search for God at Harvard* (New York: Random House, 1991), 17.

[12]H. G. Good, *A History of American Education* (New York: Macmillan, 1956), 61.

[13]Ringenberg, *The Christian College*, 38.

[14]"Yale Laws (1745)" in Cohen, *Education in the United States*, 2:675.

[15]Quoted in Hofstadter and Smith, *American Higher Education*, 1:49.

[16]"Advertisement on the Opening of Kings College," in Cohen, *Education in the United States*, 2:675.

[17]"Advertisement on the Opening of Kings College," in Cohen, *Education in the United States*, 2:675.

[18]See Gabriel Sivan, *The Bible and Civilization* (New York: Quadrangle/New York Times Book Co., 1973), 237.

[19]B.F. Morris, *The Christian Life and Character of the Civil Institutions of the United States* (Philadelphia, PA: G.W. Childs, 1864), 94.

[20]"Charter of William and Mary," in Cohen, *Education in the United States*, 2:645.

[21]Will Herberg, "Religion and Education in America," *Religious Perspectives in American Culture*, eds. James Ward Smith and A. Leland Jamison (Princeton, NJ: Princeton University Press, 1961), 12.

[22]Mark A. Noll, *A History of Christianity in the United States and Canada* (Grand Rapids, MI: Eerdmans, 1992), 365.

[23]Cited in Noll, *A History of Christianity in the United States and Canada*, 366.

[24]Cited in Noll, *A History of Christianity in the United States and Canada*, 366.

5

"IN GOD WE TRUST"

CHRISTIANITY IN OUR NATION'S CAPITOL

Samuel Adams

The official minutes of the first session of the Continental Congress in 1774 show that Sam Adams made a proposal that the sessions be opened with prayer. Not everyone agreed. John Jay and John Rutledge opposed the recommendation, claiming that the diversity of religious opinion precluded such an action. Their minority opinion did not carry the day. At the end of the debate over the proposal, Adams said that it did not become "Christian men, who had come together for solemn deliberation in the hour of their extremity, to say there was so wide a difference in their religious belief that they could not, as one man, bow the knee in prayer to the Almighty, whose advice and assistance they hoped to obtain."[1]

After the appeal by Sam Adams, the disputation ceased and Reverend Jacob Duché led in prayer. John Adams wrote home to his wife that the prayer by Duché "had an excellent effect upon everybody here. . . . Those men who were about to resort to force to obtain their rights were moved by tears" upon hearing it. The Continental Congress also issued four fast-day proclamations. The July 12, 1775, fast-day is especially significant. All the colonies were to participate. John Adams, writing to his wife from Philadelphia, said, "We have appointed a Continental fast. Millions will be upon their knees at once before the great Creator, imploring His forgiveness and blessing; His smiles on American Councils and arms."[2]

DECLARATION OF INDEPENDENCE

With the drafting of the Declaration of Independence in July of 1776, the colonies moved into a new era of political independence with ties to its Christian past. "We are endowed by our Creator with certain inalienable rights," the Declaration states. The logic is simple. No Creator, no rights.

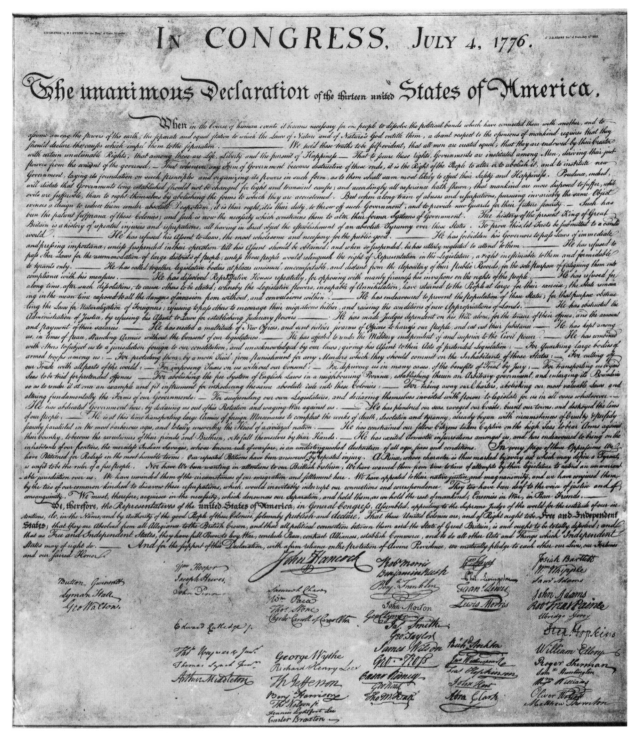

Declaration of Independence of the United States

The moral state of our nation is directly tied to this single phrase in the Declaration. Today, while people around the world clamor for rights, many in their government reject the standard by which those rights are secured. "Nature's God," the "Supreme Judge of the world," to use the language of the Declaration, makes rights a reality. One signer stated, "When I signed the Declaration of Independence I had in view, not only our independence from England, but the toleration of all sects professing the Christian religion, and communicating to them all equal rights."[3]

Drafting Committee submitting Declaration of Independence to Congress

THE CONGRESSIONAL BIBLE

In 1777 Congress issued a proclamation for a day of thanksgiving for November of that year. December 18 was also to be set aside for "solemn thanksgiving and praise." The proclamation called upon all citizens to "join the penitent confession of their manifold sins," and to offer "their humble and earnest supplication that it may please God through the merits of Jesus Christ, mercifully to forgive and blot them out of remembrance."[4]

The same year Congress issued an official resolution instructing the Committee on Commerce to import

20,000 copies of the Bible. With the outbreak of war with England, the sea lanes had been cut off to the colonies. This meant that goods that were once common in the colonies were no longer being imported—including Bibles printed in England. Congress decided to act.

The legislation of Congress on the Bible is a suggestive Christian fact, and one which evinces the faith of the statesmen of that period in its divinity, as well as their purpose to place it as the cornerstone in our republican institutions. The breaking out of the Revolution cut off the supply of "books printed in London." The scarcity of Bibles also came soon to be felt. Dr. PATRICK ALLISON, one of the chaplains to Congress, and other gentlemen, brought the subject before that body in a memorial, in which they urged the printing of an edition of the Scriptures.[5]

The committee approved the importing of 20,000 copies of the Bible from Scotland, Holland, and elsewhere. Congressmen resolved to pass this proposal because they believed "the use of the Bible is so universal, and its importance so great."[6] Even though the resolution passed, action was never taken to import the Bibles. Instead, Congress began to put emphasis on the printing of Bibles within the United States. In 1777 Robert Aitken of Philadelphia published a New Testament. Three additional editions were published. The edition of 1779 was used in schools. Aitken's efforts proved so popular that he announced his desire to publish the whole Bible. He then petitioned Congress for support. Congress adopted the following resolution in 1782:

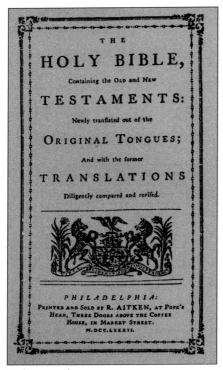

Title page of Aitken Bible

> *Resolved*, That the United States in Congress assembled, highly approve

the pious and laudable undertaking of Mr. Aitken, subservient to the interest of religion as well as the progress of the arts in this country, and being satisfied from the above report, of his care and accuracy in the execution of the work, they commend this edition of the Bible to the inhabitants of the United States, and hereby authorize him to publish this recommendation in the manner he shall think proper.[7]

The Continental Congress's records show that it was not neutral to religion. "Its records are full of references to 'God,' under many titles, to 'Jesus Christ,' the 'Christian Religion,' 'God and the Constitution,' and the 'Free Protestant Colonies.'"[8]

THE FIRST UNITED STATES CONGRESS

The first order of business of the first United States Congress was to appoint chaplains. The Right Reverend Bishop Samuel Provost and the Reverend William Linn became publicly paid chaplains of the Senate and House respectively. Since then, both the Senate and the House have continued regularly to open their sessions with prayer. Nearly all of the fifty states make some provision in their meetings for opening prayers or devotions from guest chaplains. Few if any see this as a violation of the First Amendment.

On April 30, 1789, George Washington took the oath of office with his hand on an open Bible. After taking the oath, he added, "I swear, so help me God."

Inauguration of Washington

After the resolution's adoption, Washington then issued a proclamation setting aside November 26, 1789, as a national day of thanksgiving, calling everyone to "unite in most humbly offering our prayers and supplications to the great Lord and Ruler of Nations, and beseech him to pardon our national and other transgressions."[11]

GOOD GOVERNMENT AND RELIGION

Prayers in Congress, the appointment of chaplains, and the call for days of prayers and thanksgiving do not stand alone in the historical record. The evidence is overwhelming that America has in the past always linked good government to religion—and, in particular, to Christianity. Constitutional scholars Anson Stokes and Leo Pfeffer summarize the role that the Christian religion played in the founding of this nation and the lofty position it has retained:

> Throughout its history our governments, national and state, have co-operated with religion and shown friendliness to it. God is invoked in the Declaration of Independence and in practically every state constitution. Sunday, the Christian Sabbath, is universally observed as a day of rest. The sessions of Congress and of the state legislatures are invariably opened with prayer, in Congress by chaplains who are employed by the

Following Washington's example, presidents still invoke God's name in their swearing-in ceremony.[9] The inauguration was followed by "divine services" held in St. Paul's Chapel, "performed by the Chaplain of Congress."[10] The first Congress that convened after the adoption of the Constitution requested of the President that the people of the United States observe a day of thanksgiving and prayer:

> That a joint committee of both Houses be directed to wait upon the President of the United States to request that he would recommend to the people of the United States a day of public thanksgiving and prayer, to be observed by acknowledging, with grateful hearts, the many signal favors of Almighty God, especially by affording them an opportunity peaceably to establish a Constitution of government for their safety and happiness.

FIRST PRAYER IN CONGRESS

Beautiful Reminiscence

When the Congress met, Mr Cushing made a motion that it should be opened with Prayer. It was opposed by Mr Jay, of New York, and Mr Rutledge, of South Carolina, because we were so divided in religious sentiments, some Episcopalians, some Quakers, some Anabaptists, some Presbyterians, and some Congregationalists, that we could not join in the same act of worship. Mr Samuel Adams arose and said, "that he was no bigot, and could hear a Prayer from any gentleman of Piety and virtue, who was at the same time a friend to his Country. He was a stranger in Philadelphia, but had heard that Mr Duché deserved that character, and therefore he moved that Mr Duché, an Episcopal clergyman, might be desired to read Prayers to Congress to morrow morning." The motion was seconded, and passed in the affirmative, Mr Randolph, our president, waited on Mr Duché, and received for answer, that if his health would permit, he certainly would. Accordingly next morning he appeared with his clerk, and in his pontificals, and read several Prayers in the established form, and then read the Psalter for the seventh day of September, which was the 35th Psalm. You must remember this was the next morning after we had heard the rumor of the horrible cannonade of Boston, "it seemed as if Heaven had ordained that Psalm to be read on that morning." After this, Mr Duché unexpectedly to everybody, struck out into extemporary Prayer, which filled the bosom of every man present. I must confess I never heard a better Prayer, or one so well pronounced. Episcopalian as he is, Dr Cooper himself never prayed with such fervor, such ardor, such correctness, and pathos, and in language so elegant and sublime for America, for Congress, for the Province of Massachusetts Bay, especially the town of Boston. It had excellent effect upon every body here. I must beg you to read the Psalm. If there is any faith in the sortes Virgilianae, or Homerica, or especially the sortes Biblica, it would have been thought Providential. Here was a scene worthy of the painter's art. It was in Carpenter's Hall, in Philadelphia, a building which still survives, that the devoted individuals met to whom this service was read. Washington was kneeling there, and Henry, Randolph, Rutledge, Lee, and Jay, and by their side there stood, bowed in reverence, the Puritan Patriots of New England, who at that moment had reason to believe that an armed soldiery was wasting their humble households. It was believed that Boston had been bombarded and destroyed. They prayed fervently "for America, for Congress, for the Province of Massachusetts Bay, and especially for the town of Boston," and who can realize the emotions with which they turned imploringly to Heaven for Divine interposition and aid—It was enough, says Mr Adams, to melt a heart of stone. I saw the tears gush into the eyes of the old, grave, Pacific Quakers of Phil.

ONE COUNTRY, ONE FLAG, — **ONE CONSTITUTION.**

★ PRAYER ★

The First Prayer in Congress, held in Carpenter's Hall Philadelphia was offered up by Rev. Mr. Duché Sept. 7th 1777.

Be Thou present O God of Wisdom and direct the council of this Honorable Assembly; enable them to settle all things on the best and surest foundations; that the scene of blood may be speedily closed; that Order, Harmony, and Peace may be effectually restored, and Truth, and Justice, Religion, and Piety, prevail and flourish among the people. Preserve the health of their bodies, and the vigor of their minds, shower down on them, and the millions they here represent, such temporal Blessings as Thou seest expedient for them in this world, and crown them with everlasting Glory in the world to come. All this we ask in the name and through the merits of Jesus Christ Thy Son and our Saviour. Amen.

ONE DESTINY.

First prayer in Congress held in Carpenter's Hall

Federal government. We have chaplains in our armed forces and in our penal institutions. Oaths in courts of law are administered through use of the Bible. Public officials take an oath of office ending with "so help me God." Religious institutions are tax exempt throughout the nation. Our pledge of allegiance declares that we are a nation "under God." Our national motto is "In God We Trust" and is inscribed on our currency and on some of our postage stamps.[12]

After only a cursory study of the years leading up to and including the drafting of the Constitution and the inauguration of the first president, it becomes obvious that Christianity played a foundational role in shaping our nation. It is not surprising that when courts had to define religion, they linked it to the Christian religion. In 1931, the Supreme Court declared, "We are a Christian people, according to one another the equal right of religious freedom, and acknowledging with reverence the duty of obedience to the will of God."[13] Further evidence of the role that the Christian religion played in the maintenance of our nation can be found in national pronouncements and inscriptions in our nation's capital.

OFFICIAL ACTS OF CONGRESS AND THE PRESIDENT

1. Our nation's coins have not always had "In God We Trust" stamped on them. In 1862 many people began to request that our coinage make reference to God. A sermon by the Reverend Henry Augustus Boardman of Philadelphia declared that "The coinage of the United States is without a God."[14] Some suggested "God our Trust." In 1863 the motto "God and our Country" was proposed. The motto "In God We Trust" appeared for the first time in 1864 and received formal Congressional approval the following year. On March 3, 1865, Congress enacted the following:

> *And be it further enacted*, That, in addition to the devices and legends upon the gold, silver, and other coins of the United States, it shall be lawful for the director of the mint, with the approval of the Secretary of the Treasury, to cause the motto "In God we trust" to be placed upon such coins hereafter to be issued as shall admit of such legend thereon.[15]

The motto also was placed on the silver dollar, half-dollar and quarter-dollar coins and on the five-cent coin, beginning in 1866. The interest to secure a place for the motto was high because of the events of the civil war. Repentance and trust in God were themes that echoed through the nation after the blood of so many had been shed.

The motto was temporarily dropped in 1907, when President Theodore Roosevelt commissioned the American sculpture Augustus Saint-Gaudens to design new coins, a design that did not include "In God We Trust." The matter came before Congress on May 18, 1908, and an act was passed to restore the motto. "In 1955 Congress extended the act by requiring the phrase to appear not only on all coins, but on all paper money thereafter minted or printed. The next year, 1956, Congress enacted a law making the phrase 'In God We Trust' officially the national motto."[16]

2. The President is authorized to proclaim at least two National Days of Prayer each year. Public Law 82-324 requires the President to proclaim a National Day of Prayer on a day other than a Sunday. Under Public Law 77-379 the President proclaims the fourth Thursday of November each year as a National Day of Thanksgiving.

3. The words "under God" were inserted into the Pledge of Allegiance by an act of Congress in 1954. The House and Senate adopted the measure without a dissenting vote. On June 14 of that same year, President Dwight D. Eisenhower stood on the steps of the Capitol Building and, for the first time, recited the revised pledge to the flag that included the phrase "one nation under God."[17]

4. On April 30, 1863, President Abraham Lincoln appointed a "National Fast Day." It reads in part: "It is the duty of nations as well as of men to own their dependence upon the overruling power of God, to confess their sins and transgressions in humble sorrow, yet with assured hope that genuine repentance will lead to mercy and pardon, and to recognize the sublime truth, announced in the Holy Scriptures and proven by all history: that those nations only are blessed whose God is the Lord."[18]

5. Congress declared 1983 to be the "Year of the Bible." The declaration read in part: "The Bible, the Word of God, has made a unique contribution in shaping the United States as a distinctive and blessed nation. . . . Deeply held religious convictions springing from the Holy Scriptures led to the early settlement of our Nation. . . . Biblical teaching inspired concepts of civil government that are contained in our Declaration of Independence and the Constitution of the United States" (Public Law 97-280, 96 Stat. 1211, approved October 4, 1982).

U.S. Supreme Court

6. When the Supreme Court convenes and the chief justice and associate justices stand before their desks, the marshal makes an ascription to Almighty God in the Court Call saying, "God save the United States and this honorable court."

7. The same year that Congress approved adding the phrase "under God" to the Pledge of Allegiance, both houses passed a resolution directing the Capitol architect to make available "a room, with facilities for prayer and meditation, for the use of members of the Senate and House of

Representatives."[19] The seventh edition of *The Capitol*, an official publication of the United States Congress, gives the following description:

The history that gives this room its inspirational lift is centered in the stained glass window. George Washington kneeling in prayer . . . is the focus of the composition. . . . Behind Washington a prayer is etched: "Preserve me, O God, for in Thee do I put my trust," the first verse of the sixteenth Psalm. There are upper and lower medallions representing the two sides of the Great Seal of the United States. On these are inscribed the phrases: *annuit coeptis*—"God has favored our undertakings"—and *novus ordo seclorum*—"A new order of the ages is born." Under the upper medallion is the phrase from Lincoln's immortal Gettysburg Address, "This Nation under God.". . . The two lower corners of the window each show the Holy Scriptures, an open book and a candle, signifying the light from God's law, "Thy Word is a lamp unto my feet and a light unto my path" [Psalm 119:105].[20]

The prayer room is decidedly Christian in character. The Bible is featured, not the Book of Mormon. Religious citations are taken from the Bible. Subsequent editions of *The Capitol* book no longer contain the material on the congressional prayer room. While there is a picture of the room in a later edition, a description of its religious features is absent.

Stained glass window with verse and Washington praying in the Congressional Prayer Room in Washington, D.C.

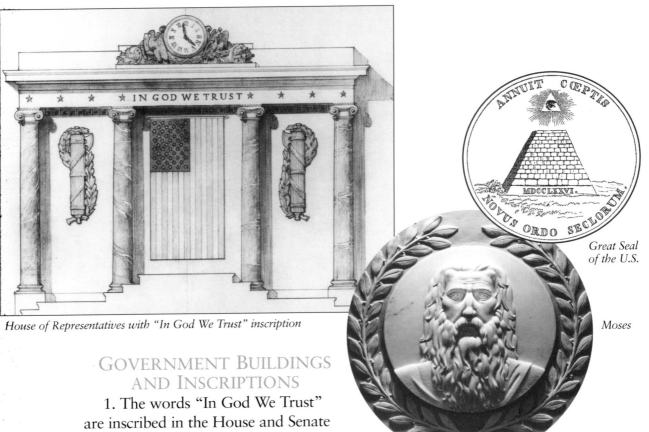

House of Representatives with "In God We Trust" inscription

Great Seal of the U.S.

Moses

GOVERNMENT BUILDINGS AND INSCRIPTIONS

1. The words "In God We Trust" are inscribed in the House and Senate chambers.

2. On the walls of the Capitol dome, these words appear: "The New Testament according to the Lord and Savior Jesus Christ."

3. In the Rotunda of the Capitol is the figure of the crucified Christ.

4. "The Baptism of Pocahontas at Jamestown" (1613) hangs in the Capitol Rotunda.

5. The "Embarkation of the Pilgrims" (1620) shows Elder William Brewster holding a Bible opened to the title page which reads "The New Testament of Our Lord and Savior Jesus Christ." The words "God With Us" are inscribed on the sail of the ship. This painting also hangs in the Rotunda of the Capitol.

6. A relief of Moses hangs in the House Chamber. Moses is surrounded by twenty-two other lawgivers.

7. The Latin phrase *Annuit Coeptis*, "[God] has smiled on our undertaking," is inscribed on the Great Seal of the United States.

8. Under the Seal is the phrase from Lincoln's Gettysburg address: "This nation under God."

9. The Liberty Bell has Leviticus 25:10 prominently displayed in a band around its top: "Proclaim liberty throughout all the land, unto the inhabitants thereof."

10. President Eliot of Harvard chose Micah 6:8 for the walls of the Library of Congress: "He hath showed thee, O man, what is good; and what doth God require of thee, but to do justly, and to love mercy, and to walk humbly with thy God."

11. The lawmaker's library quotes the Psalmist's acknowledgment of the beauty and order of creation: "The heavens declare the glory of God, and the firmament showeth His handiwork" (Psalm 19:1).

12. Engraved on the metal cap on the top of the Washington Monument are the words: "Praise be to God."

Lining the walls of the stairwell are numerous Bible verses: "Search the Scriptures" (John 5:39), "Holiness to the Lord," and "Train up a child in the way he should go, and when he is old he will not depart from it" (Prov. 22:6).

13. The crier who opens each session of the Supreme Court closes with the words, "God save the United States and the Honorable Court."

14. At the opposite end of the Lincoln Memorial, words and phrases from Lincoln's Second Inaugural Address allude to "God," the "Bible," "providence," "the Almighty," and "divine attributes."

15. A plaque in the Dirksen Office Building has the words "IN GOD WE TRUST" in bronze relief.

16. The Jefferson Memorial includes these words from Thomas Jefferson: "God who gave us life gave us liberty. Can the liberties of a nation be secure when we have removed a conviction that these liberties are the gift of God? Indeed I tremble for my country when I reflect that God is just, that his justice cannot sleep forever."

17. Each president takes his oath of office with his left hand placed on an open Bible and concludes the oath with these words: "So help me God." The Senate doors (bronze) show George Washington taking the presidential oath with his hands on a Bible.

Liberty Bell

CONCLUSION

It makes a difference that our coins are stamped with "In God We Trust" instead of "In Allah We Trust." It's important to note that the Library of Congress has a quotation from a Psalm, instead of a line from the Quran or the Book of Mormon. In addition, it's significant to note that "every foreigner attests his renunciation of allegiance to his former sovereign and his acceptance of citizenship in this republic by an appeal to God."[21]

History is on the side of those who claim that America's founding was Christian, from its fragile historical documents to its declarations engraved in stone.

But as true as these symbols may be, and as important as our structures may be, they are not, in and of themselves, evidence or assurance of America's greatness—past, present, or future. National greatness does not spring from an accumulation of archival antiquities and architectural details, or from symbols and slogans. It does not spring from documents, precedents, constitutions, or legislation. National greatness springs from righteousness, goodness, character, and true spirituality![22]

As Scripture declares: "Righteousness exalts a nation, but sin is a reproach to any people" (Proverbs 14:34 NKJV) and "A throne is established by righteousness" (16:12 NKJV). It is these declarations that should be engraved on our hearts and signify the true heritage of a nation.

[1]Quoted in Key Paton, "Notable Chaplains," *Eternity* (November 1986), 28.

[2]Anson Phelps Stokes and Leo Pfeffer, *Church and State in the United States* (New York: Harper & Row, 1964), 83.

[3]Quoted in Stokes and Pfeffer, *Church and State in the United States*, 85.

[4]Quoted in Stokes and Pfeffer, *Church and State in the United States*, 83-84.

[5]B. F. Morris, *The Christian Life and Character of the Civil Institutions of the United States* (Philadelphia, PA: G.W. Childs, 1864), 215.

[6]From a report submitted to Congress, quoted in John Wright, *Early Bibles in America*, 3rd rev. ed. (New York: Thomas Whittaker, 1894), 55.

[7]Quoted in Wright, *Early Bibles in America*, 58.

[8]Stokes and Pfeffer, *Church and State in the United States*, 86.

[9]Richard G. Hutcheson, Jr., *God in the White House: How Religion Has Changed the Modern Presidency* (New York: Macmillan, 1988), 37.

[10]Stokes and Pfeffer, *Church and State in the United States*, 87.

[11]Quoted in Stokes and Pfeffer, *Church and State in the United States*, 87.

[12]Stokes and Pfeffer, *Church and State in the United States*, 102-103.

[13]*United States vs. Macintosh*, 283 U.S. 625 (1931).

[14]Quoted in Stokes and Pfeffer, *Church and State in the United States*, 568.

[15]Quoted in Stokes and Pfeffer, *Church and State in the United States*, 568.

[16]Stokes and Pfeffer, *Church and State in the United States*, 570. Complete information can be found online at www.ustreas.gov/opc/opc0011.html.

[17]Much of the material in this section is taken from the seventh edition (1979) of *The Capitol* (Washington D.C.: United States Government Printing Office, 1979), 24-25.

[18]Abraham Lincoln, "Proclamation Appointing a National Fast Day," April 30, 1863, *The Collected Works of Abraham Lincoln*, ed. Roy P. Bassler (New Brunswick, NJ: Rutgers University Press, 1953), 6:155-56.

[19]*The Prayer Room of the United States Capitol*, booklet published by the U.S. Printing Office, 1956.

[20]*The Capitol*, 25.

[21]David J. Brewer, *The United States: A Christian Nation* (Philadelphia, PA: The John C. Winston Co., 1905), 31.

[22]Peter J. Leithart and George Grant, *In Defense of Greatness: How Biblical Character Shapes a Nation's Destiny* (Ft. Lauderdale, FL: Coral Ridge Ministries, 1990), 4.

6

THE SEPARATION MYTH

CHRISTIANITY AND THE FIRST AMENDMENT

First Amendment to the Constitution of the United States

Does the First Amendment require a secular government? Is the First Amendment violated when Christians apply biblical principles to public policy issues? Too many debates over the meaning of the First Amendment are confused by a failure to cite it accurately or comprehensively: "Congress shall make no law respecting an establishment of religion, or prohibiting the free exercise thereof; or abridging the freedom of speech or of the press; or the right of the people peaceably to assemble, and to petition the Government for a redress of grievances." An accurate interpretation of the amendment must include the following:

- There is no mention of the words "Church," "State," or "separation" in the First Amendment.

- Included in the amendment are additional rights which relate to the free exercise of religion: the right to talk about religion (freedom of speech), the right to publish religious works (freedom of the press), the right of people to worship publicly, either individually or in groups (freedom of assembly), and the right to petition the government when it goes beyond its delegated constitutional authority in these areas (the right of political involvement).

- The prohibition in the First Amendment is addressed exclusively to *Congress*. Individual states and governmental institutions (e.g., public schools, Capitol building steps, national parks, etc.) are not included in the amendment's prohibition. As clear as this is, some try to rewrite the First Amendment in order to fit their misconceptions about its meaning and implementation. One way is to make the amendment apply to the states, as in this example: "The First

Amendment to the U.S. Constitution is the direct descendant of Jefferson's Virginia resolution, and its words are quite clear. Congress, and by extension the states, 'shall make no law respecting an establishment of religion.'"[1] If the constitutional framers wanted to include the phrase "and *by extension the states*," they would have done so. Since the states insisted on including a Bill of Rights to protect them, why would they include an amendment that restricted their sovereignty?

• There is no mention of a freedom *from* religion. The First Amendment offers no support of a position that would outlaw religion just because it exists or offends those of a different religion or those who have no religion at all.

• There is a second part to the religion clause of the First Amendment that states that Congress cannot "prohibit the free exercise thereof." In a June 19, 2000, ruling by the Supreme Court, the majority of justices outlawed student-led prayer at high school sporting events. For example, a teacher of political science and constitutional law at Agnes Scott College in Decatur, Georgia, in support of the Court's decision, never quotes the clause that mandates that there can be *no prohibition* of "the free exercise of religion."[2]

With so much debate, how does anyone know what the First Amendment really means? An interpreter of any document as important as the Constitution must consider the historical circumstances that led to its formation, the vocabulary of the period, documents of similar construction, the political views of the authors, the prevailing religious worldview, and the intended audience. With these points in mind, it would be wise, therefore, to follow the method suggested by Thomas Jefferson in understanding the *original meaning* of the First Amendment:

> On every question of construction, carry ourselves back to the time when the Constitution was adopted, recollect the spirit manifested in the debates, and instead of trying what meaning may be squeezed out of the text, or invented against it, conform to the probable one in which it was passed.[3]

James Wilson (1742-1798), one of only six men who signed both the Declaration of Independence and the Constitution, and who also served on the Supreme Court, offered similar sound advice. "The first and governing maxim in the interpretation of a statute is to discover the meaning of those who made it." As Oliver Wendell Holmes put it, "A page of history is worth a volume of logic."[4]

Oliver Wendell Holmes

THE AMENDMENT'S HISTORY

With this brief introduction, let's look into the history behind this much referred to, but often misquoted, misunderstood, and misapplied amendment. When the Constitution was sent to the states for ratification, there was fear that the new national government had too much power. It was then proposed that additional prohibitions should be listed in the Constitution to restrict further the national government's power and authority.

The area of religion was important, since a number of the states had established churches. Some of the framers were concerned that the federal government would establish a *national* church (e.g., Anglican, Presbyterian, or Congregational) to be funded by tax dollars and controlled by the newly formed government, and that a national church would disestablish the existing state churches. So then, the First Amendment was designed to protect the *states* against the national (federal) government. The amendment was not designed to disestablish the Christian religion as it found expression in the state constitutions or anywhere else. Justice Joseph Story, a Supreme Court justice of the nineteenth century, offers the following commentary on the amendment's original meaning:

The real object of the First Amendment was not to countenance, much less to advance Mohammedanism, or Judaism, or infidelity, by prostrating Christianity, but to exclude all rivalry among Christian sects [denominations] and to prevent any national ecclesiastical establishment which would give to an hierarchy the exclusive patronage of the national government.[5]

Story's comments are important. He states that the amendment's purpose was "to exclude all rivalry among Christian sects." This assessment presupposes that Christianity was the accepted religion of the colonies, but that no single sect should be mandated by law. The amendment was not designed to make all religions equal, only to make all *Christian* denominations (sects) equal in the eyes of the Constitution and the law.

THE ESTABLISHMENT CLAUSE

The word "establishment," as used in the First Amendment, means recognition by civil government of a single denomination as the official State Church. The amendment does not prohibit *the* establishment of religion in general, but *rather an* establishment of

Justice Joseph Story

a particular Christian denomination, which our founders called a "sect." Furthermore, there is nothing in the First Amendment restricting the states. The restriction only applies to Congress: "*Congress* shall make no law." Writing the minority opinion in the *Wallace v. Jaffree* case (1985), Supreme Court Justice William Rehnquist stated, "The Framers intended the Establishment Clause to prohibit the designation of any church as a 'national' one. The clause was also designed to stop the Federal government from asserting a preference for one religious denomination or sect over others."[6]

George Washington

If the amendment had been constructed to remove religion from having an impact on civil governmental issues, then it would seem rather strange that on September 24, 1789, the same day it approved the First Amendment, Congress called on President Washington to proclaim a national day of prayer and thanksgiving which read:

> That a joint committee of both Houses be directed to wait upon the President of the United States to request that he would recommend to the people of the United States a day of public thanksgiving and prayer, to be observed by acknowledging, with grateful hearts, the many signal favors of Almighty God, especially by affording them an opportunity peaceably to establish a Constitution of government for their safety and happiness.[7]

This proclamation acknowledges "the many signal favors of Almighty God, especially by *affording them an opportunity peaceably to establish a Constitution of government for their safety and happiness.*" This is odd language for a group of men who supposedly just separated religion from government at all levels. In fact, this resolution uses devoutly religious language to acknowledge that they would not even have a government without God's blessing.

Roger Williams

HISTORICAL FICTION

The origin of the "separation between Church and State" phrase has two sources. The first is in the writings of Roger Williams, founder of Rhode Island. The most noted reference, however, is in a letter Thomas Jefferson wrote to a group of Baptist pastors in Danbury, Connecticut, in 1802. In that letter Jefferson wrote:

> Believing with you that religion is a matter which lies solely between

man and his God, that he owes account to none other for faith or his worship, that the legislative powers of government reach actions only, and not opinions, I contemplate with sovereign reverence that act of the whole American people which declared that their legislature should "make no law respecting an establishment of religion, or prohibiting the free exercise thereof," thus building a wall of separation between church and state.[8]

Jefferson had no hand in the drafting of the Constitution or the Bill of Rights. He was in France at the time. While Jefferson's opinions are instructive, they remain opinions. His personal correspondence, even as President, has no legal standing. In addition, Jefferson's use of the phrase "separation between church and state" is "a mere metaphor too vague to support any theory of the Establishment Clause."[9] Yet, it is Jefferson's vague "metaphor" that has been adopted as the standard substitute for the actual language of the First Amendment.

When he was governor of Virginia, Jefferson readily issued proclamations declaring days of "public and solemn thanksgiving and prayer to Almighty God."[10] Jefferson's Virginia "Bill for Punishing Disturbers of Religious

Thomas Jefferson

Worship and Sabbath Breakers," was introduced by James Madison in the Virginia Assembly in 1785 and became law in 1786. The section on Sabbath desecration reads:

> If any person on Sunday shall himself be found labouring at his own or any other trade or calling, or shall employ his apprentices, servants or slaves in labour, or other business, except it be in the ordinary household offices of daily necessity, or other work of necessity or charity, he shall forfeit the sum of ten shillings for every such offence, deeming every apprentice, servant, or slave so employed, and every day he shall be so employed as constituting a distinct offence.[11]

As president, Jefferson included a prayer in each of his two inaugural addresses. He signed bills appropriating money for chaplains in Congress and the armed services and signed the Articles of War, which not only provided for chaplains, but also "earnestly recommended to all officers and soldiers, diligently to attend divine services."[12] In 1803, Jefferson signed an appropriation of funds to be paid to the Kaskaskia Indians, who "in part, called for the United States to build them a Roman Catholic Church and pay their priest."[13]

Jefferson advocated that the tax-supported College of William and Mary maintain "a perpetual mission among the Indian tribes" which included the instruction of "the principles of Christianity." Jefferson's proposed curriculum for the University of Virginia included a provision for a "professor of ethics" who would present "the Proofs of the being of God, the Creator, Preserver, and Supreme Ruler of the universe, the Author of all the relations of morality, and of the laws and obligations these infer."[14] While Jefferson was against ecclesiastical control of education, he was not against the teaching of religion in state-supported institutions.

Along with Benjamin Franklin, Jefferson proposed that the design for the nation's seal should include the biblical image of Pharoah's army being destroyed as it passed through the Red Sea. The banner "Rebellion to Tyrants is Obedience to God" was to circle the overtly religious image.

In his Second Inaugural Address (1805), Jefferson stated, "In matters of religion I have considered that its free exercise is placed by the Constitution independent of the powers of the General Government. I have therefore undertaken on no occasion to prescribe the religious exercises suited to it, but have left them, as the Constitution found them, under the direction and discipline of the church or

First Design for Seal

state authorities acknowledged by the several religious societies."[15] According to Jefferson, the federal ("General") Government has no jurisdiction over churches or state governments. "Many contemporary writers attempt to read back into the past a 'wall of separation' between church and state which, in fact, never has existed in the United States."[16]

THE NORTHWEST ORDINANCE

The meaning of the First Amendment, as history will attest, has nothing to do with separating the moral aspects of the Christian religion from civil affairs. The Northwest Ordinance of 1787, enacted by the Continental Congress and reenacted by the newly formed federal government in 1789, after it had agreed on the final wording of the First Amendment, stated that "good government" must be based on some moral foundation: "Religion, morality and knowledge, being necessary to good government and the happiness of mankind, schools and the means of education shall be forever encouraged."

The First Congress did not expect the Bill of Rights to be inconsistent with the Northwest Ordinance of 1787, which the Congress reenacted in 1789. One key clause in the

Ordinance explained why Congress chose to set aside some of the federal lands in the territory for schools: "Religion, morality, and knowledge," the clause read, "being necessary to good government and the happiness of mankind, schools and the means of learning shall forever be encouraged." This clause clearly implies that schools, which were to be built on federal lands with federal assistance, were expected to promote religion as well as morality. In fact, most schools at this time were church-run sectarian schools.[17]

Constitutional scholar Leo Pfeffer writes, "[F]or all practical purposes, Christianity and religion were synonymous."[18] It is clear that our Founders never supposed that moral precepts founded on the Christian religion should be excluded from policy making, even though they worked diligently to keep the institutions and jurisdictions of Church and State separate.

Strict separationists do not see the Northwest Ordinance as convincing evidence that the constitutional framers regarded religion, politics, and morality as an acceptable mix. Robert Boston, an absolute separationist, asserts that if the Founders had wanted to support religion, the Northwest Ordinance would have ended, ". . . schools and *churches* shall forever be encouraged."[19] Boston assumes that since the delegates did not call for the support of churches that this meant they were opposed to mixing religion and politics. The source of Boston's confusion comes from the "tendency to employ the words 'Church' and 'religion' as synonyms. To maintain that there must be a separation between Church and State does not necessarily mean that there must be a separation between religion and State."[20]

I wonder how the ACLU would react to the Northwest Ordinance if its principles were applied to today's public schools? Lawyers would be immediately dispatched to assert that the Ordinance was unconstitutional because it mixes religion and morality with public education. Those in Jefferson's day did not find a problem with this combination, either constitutionally or practically.

CONCLUSION

The First Amendment "provides a *legal* separation between Church and State: *not a moral nor a spiritual* separation. . . . There is no reason, under the Constitution of the United States, why the principles of Christianity cannot pervade the laws and institutions of the United States of America."[21]

Today's Christian political activists are not calling on the State to establish churches, to force people to attend church, or to pay for the work of the church. They are simply maintaining that we cannot have good government without a moral foundation, and that moral foundation resides in the Christian religion.

[1]Editorial Page, *Atlanta Constitution* (November 15, 1994), A18.

[2]Gus Cochran, "Court rightfully tosses prayers," *Atlanta Constitution* (June 20, 2000), A9.

[3]Letter to Justice William Johnson, Monticello, June 12, 1823. See Thomas Jefferson, *Thomas Jefferson: Writings* (Autobiography, Notes on the State of Virginia, Public and Private Papers, Addresses, Letters) (New York: The Library of America, 1984), 1475

[4]*New York Trust Co. v. Eisner*, 256 U.S. 345, 349 (1921). Quoted in Daniel L. Dreisbach, *Real Threat and Mere Shadow: Religious Liberty and the First Amendment* (Westchester, IL: Crossway Books, 1987), xiii.

[5]Quoted by Judge Brevard Hand, in *Jaffree vs. Board of School Commissioners of Mobile County*, 544 F. Supp. 1104 (S. D. Ala. 1983) in Russell Kirk, ed., *The Assault on Religion: Commentaries on the Decline of Religious Liberty* (Lanham, NY: University Press of America, 1986), 84.

[6]*Wallace v. Jaffree*, 472 U.S., 113. Jude P. Dougherty, "Separating Church and State," *The World & I* (December 1987), 686.

[7]*The Annals of the Congress, The Debates and Proceedings in the Congress of the United States*, Compiled From Authentic Materials by Joseph Gales, Senior (Washington, D.C.: Gales and Seaton, 1834), 1:949-50.

[8]Quoted in Charles E. Rice, *The Supreme Court and Public Prayer: The Need for Restraint* (New York: Fordham University Press, 1964), 63.

[9]Peter J. Ferrara, *Religion and the Constitution: A Reinterpretation* (Washington, D.C.: Free Congress Foundation, 1983), 34-35.

[10]Quoted in Rice, *The Supreme Court and Public Prayer*, 63.

[11]"A Bill for Punishing Disturbers of Religious Worship and Sabbath Breakers," in Julian P. Boyd, ed., *The Papers of Thomas Jefferson* (Princeton, NJ: Princeton University Press, 1950), Vol. 2, 1777 to June 18, 1779, including the Revisal of the Laws, 1776-1786, 555. Robert L. Cord, *Separation of Church and State: Historical Fact and Current Fiction* (Grand Rapids, MI: Baker Book House, [1982] 1988), 217.

[12]Act of April 10, 1806, C. 20, 2 Stat. 359, 360. Quoted in Rice, *The Supreme Court and Public Prayer*, 63-64.

[13]Cord, "Church-State Separation and the Public Schools," 28.

[14]"Bill for the Establishment of District Colleges and University" (1817). Quoted in Charles Wesley Lowry, *To Pray or Not to Pray!: A Handbook for Study of Recent Supreme Court Decisions and American Church-State Doctrine* (Washington, DC: University Press of Washington D.C., 1963), 38-39.

[15]Thomas Jefferson, "Second Inaugural Address," in James D. Richardson, ed., *A Compilation of the Messages and Papers of the Presidents, 1789-1902*, 12 vols. (Washington, DC: Bureau of National Literature and Art, 1907), 1:379-80.

[16]Franklin Hamlin Littell, *From State Church to Pluralism: A Protestant Interpretation of Religion in American History* (Chicago, IL: Aldine Publishing Co., 1962), 99.

[17]Michael J. Malbin, *Religion and Politics: The Intentions of the Authors of the First Amendment* (Washington, D.C.: American Enterprise Institute for Public Policy Research, 1978), 14-15.

[18]Leo Pfeffer, *Church, State and Freedom* (Boston, MA: Beacon Press, 1953), 98.

[19]Robert Boston, *Why the Religious Right Is Wrong about Separation of Church and State* (Buffalo, NY: Prometheus Books, 1993), 80.

[20]J. Marcellus Kik, *Church and State: The Story of Two Kingdoms* (New York: Thomas Nelson & Sons, 1963), 124.

[21]Kik, *Church and State*, 116.

7

THE TEN COMMANDMENTS ON TRIAL

A SUPREME LEGAL FIGHT

"Ladies and Gentlemen, young and old. This may seem an unusual procedure, speaking to you before the picture begins, but we have an unusual subject: the birth of freedom. The story of Moses." Yes, it was an unusual way to begin a movie. The introductory words were spoken by Cecil B. de Mille, the director of *The Ten Commandments* (1956). But de Mille had something more in mind than just making a movie. He considered his production to be so important that he came out on stage to deliver a short but powerful statement on the nature of freedom under the law of God:

> The theme of this picture is whether men ought to be ruled by God's laws or whether they are to be ruled by the whims of a dictator like Rameses. Are men the property of the State or are they free souls under God? This same battle continues throughout the world today.[1]

All law is a reflection of some world-view.[2] It is impossible to avoid legislating morality. Laws against theft and murder are legislated, and they reflect some moral code. There are few people who would object to laws being made that would punish thieves and murderers. And yet, such laws impose a moral system on all of us. Although thieves and murderers might object, no one is calling for these laws to be rescinded because they impose a moral code:

Richmond County, GA Court Seal

> Every system of government exists to produce or enforce certain laws, and every law necessarily entails a set of moral assumptions. All morality—even that which is usually supposed to be, or touted as being, based upon an "irreligious" or "anti-religious" philosophical foundation—is ultimately religious in its nature, since it is founded upon a set of pretheoretical presuppositions, fundamental assumptions about the nature of reality, about God, man, and things, which are taken on (a usually unacknowledged) faith. In this deepest sense, then, the question for every legal system is not whether it will be based upon "religion" but rather which religion or religious philosophy will be its foundation?[3]

69

The Sermon on the Mount

The fundamental basis of this nation's laws was given to Moses on the Mount. The fundamental basis of our Bill of Rights comes from the teachings which we get from Exodus and St. Matthew, from Isaiah and St. Paul. I don't think we comprehend that enough these days.

If we don't have the proper fundamental moral background, we will finally wind up with a totalitarian government which does not believe in rights for anybody.[4]

How times and laws have changed.

THE ROOTS OF MORALITY

If morality is not rooted in God's character, then it's found in man, the mob, or the State. When God is expelled from the cosmos, atheism, a belief system in its own right, becomes the new god. Barbara Reynolds, a columnist for *USA Today,* understands the consequences of abandoning God and His laws as a fixed moral standard. The only other option is "an atheistic, belligerent tone" that results in oppression:

Prohibiting the teaching of creationism in favor of evolution creates an atheistic, belligerent tone that might explain why our kids sometimes perform like Godzilla instead of children made in the image of God.

While evolution teaches that we are accidents or freaks of nature, creationism shows humankind as the offspring of a divine Creator. There are rules to follow which govern not only our time on Earth, but also our afterlife.

One system of morality is set against another in the debate over legislation. Moral persuasion is always used. "It is immoral to allow people to live in cardboard boxes or in abandoned automobiles when there is so much wealth in a country like the United States," advocates for the homeless claim. Champions of peace push their cause with, "It's immoral to make bombs when there are so many needy people in the world."

These moral crusaders work for change at every level of government to secure legislative support for their cause. Moral arguments are always used. But how do we know what's moral? President Harry S. Truman voiced the common and prevailing sentiment:

If evolution is forced on our kids, we shouldn't be perplexed when they beat on their chests or, worse yet, beat on each other and their teachers.[5]

Reynolds's comments are reminiscent of what C.S. Lewis wrote: "We make men without chests and we expect of them virtue and enterprise. We laugh at honor and we are shocked to find traitors in our midst. We castrate and bid the geldings be fruitful."[6] We strip men and women of the certainty that they are created in the image of God, and we are surprised when they act like the beasts of the field.

THE START OF A CAMPAIGN

For more than a century, starting with the publication of Charles Darwin's *On the Origin of Species* in 1859, America has been slowly moving away from the nation's original biblical foundation with disastrous results. Astute students of history are well aware of the devastating effects the rejection of God's law has had on our nation. Some saw it earlier than others.

In St. Cloud, Minnesota, in 1946, juvenile-court judge E.J. Ruegemer confronted a defiant 16-year-old boy accused of stealing a car and causing an accident.

The judge asked the young man if he realized he had broken the Ten Commandments. The boy admitted that he never even heard of the Ten Commandments. Shocked at the teenager's ignorance, Judge Ruegemer took out a Bible, handed it to him, and told him his sentence was to learn the Ten Commandments and obey them.

"I decided to give him a chance; he can't follow laws he doesn't know," said Judge Ruegemer.

The incident prompted the judge to mount a campaign to place prints of the Ten Commandments in courthouses across the nation to serve for the guidance of defendants. He approached the Fraternal Order of Eagles for help in getting the message out. The service organization was inundated with orders from cities across the country.

Moses and the Ten Commandments

"I thought that if the commandments could be placed in courtrooms, then judges could point them out to offenders," he said.[7]

When de Mille heard of Judge Ruegemer's earlier campaign, he decided to make a more permanent statement. With the release of his classic *Ten Commandments* film in 1956, de Mille promoted it by placing etched granite slabs of the commandments in parks, state-capital lawns, and courthouses around the country. Counts vary, but it's estimated that "4,000 Ten Commandment monuments are displayed in U.S. cities."[8] These monuments and other representations of the Ten Commandments have come under legal scrutiny by the American Civil Liberties Union (ACLU) and the courts for their supposed violation of the First Amendment to the Constitution.

THE TEN COMMANDMENTS AND THE SUPREME COURT

What began as a moral crusade and a motion picture promotion has turned into a supreme legal fight. In Richmond County, Georgia, a fight has ensued over the court seal which includes an image that resembles the two tables of the law, the Ten Commandments. The ACLU claims that these types of images "violate constitutional church-state separation."[9] In another similar case, the ACLU sent a disapproving letter to the mayor of Ringgold, Georgia, explaining why the display in City Hall was unconstitutional: They "are fundamentally religious in nature and when displayed by the government, convey the city's endorsement of religion in general and Christianity in particular."[10] Such displays are popping up around the country again, from Alabama, Kentucky, and Indiana to South Dakota, Pennsylvania, and Missouri. And as quickly as they go up, the ACLU is just as quick with a threat to sue to have them taken down.

When Judge Roy Moore ran for the office of chief justice of the Alabama Supreme Court, he made a pledge to restore America's moral foundation. He began to deliver on his promise when he placed a 5,280-pound granite monument of the Ten Commandments in the rotunda of the state Judicial Building.

Display of Ten Commandments in the rotunda of the State Judicial Building in Montgomery, Alabama

Supreme Court marble frieze showing Moses with Ten Commandments

The monument also included the phrase from the Declaration of Independence, "the Laws of Nature and of Nature's God"; the national Motto, "In God We Trust"; the Pledge of Allegiance, "One Nation Under God"; and the Judicial Oath, "So Help Me God." During the brief ceremony dedicating the monument, Judge Moore made these summary comments: "May this day mark the beginning of the restoration of the moral foundation of law to our people and a return to the knowledge of God in our land."[11]

THE LAW ETCHED IN STONE

Who's right in the battle over the Ten Commandments? If, as the ACLU maintains, the posting of the Ten Command-ments is "fundamentally religious" and the "endorsement of religion in general and Christianity in particular," doesn't this mean that the displays are by definition unconstitutional? Ultimately, a ruling would have to come from the Supreme Court. But how would the Court rule once it learns that displays of the Ten Commandments have such a long history without any legal challenge? For example, a visitor who enters the National Archives to view the original Constitution, Declaration of Independence, and other official documents must first pass by a copy of the Ten Commandments prominently displayed in the entryway to the Archives.

An allegorical representation of the Ten Commandments

The justices might be surprised to learn that the Supreme Court building itself has four displays of the Ten Commandments, three of which are carved in stone:

• The Ten Commandments are engraved on the lower half of two large oak doors as you enter the Chamber.

• A marble frieze in the Chamber itself shows Moses holding a copy of the Ten Commandments inscribed in Hebrew.

• Two allegorical figures, representing "The Power of Government" and "The Majesty of Government," stand beside a carved flat-faced tablet with two rows of Roman numerals, I-V and VI-X, an obvious rendering of the Ten Commandments.

• Just above the place where the Chief Justice sits, a carved stone ban-ner reads "Justice, the Guardian of Liberty." Centered above the banner, a seated Moses is shown holding a copy of the Ten Commandments.

As Chief Justice Warren Burger noted in his majority opinion of *Lynch v. Donnelly* (1984), the Supreme Court Chamber in which cases related to reli-gion are "heard is decorated with a notable and permanent–not seasonal–symbol of religion: Moses with the Ten Commandments."[12]

In addition to the Supreme Court, state courtrooms and capitols across our land have housed similar displays for decades without any legal challenges or constitutional prohibitions: The Texas State Capitol, the chambers of the Pennsylvania Supreme Court, and scores of other legislatures, courthouses, and other public buildings. "In fact, the Ten Commandments are more easily found in America's government buildings than in her religious buildings, thus demonstrating the understanding by generations of Americans from coast to coast that the Ten Commandments formed the basis of America's civil laws."[13]

One of the most interesting displays is a sixteen-panel mural painted by Violet Oakley that graces the walls of the courtroom of the Supreme Court in the Capitol Building in Harrisburg, Pennsylvania. The panels show the progress of law, "beginning with the panel of Divine Law, over the entrance door, and ending with the Spirit of the Law, so beautifully symbolized by

Mural of Moses and Ten Commandments in Pennsylvania Supreme Court

Christ walking upon a troubled sea filled with sinking ships of strife."[14] Another panel shows Jesus Christ, in the Sermon on the Mount, revealing the Christian idea of Law. One of the most striking panels displays, in the words of the artist, "Moses hewing out the Ten Commandments upon Mount Sinai, under divine inspiration."[15]

In a summary statement of the relationship between Divine Law, Natural Law, the Common Law, and the Law of Reason, the artist includes panels that are illuminated with quotations from the introduction to Sir William Blackstone's *Commentaries on the Laws of England*. Blackstone and his *Commentaries* had the profoundest impact on American law. According to Blackstone, "Human laws are only declaratory of an act in subordination to Divine Law."

How can the ACLU maintain that displays of the Ten Commandments violate the First Amendment when these Christian depictions of law were commissioned, sanctioned, and presided over by the State Supreme Court of Pennsylvania in the 1920s? If the ACLU and today's courts are consistent, these murals will have to be covered up or painted over. When a copy of the mural showing Moses with the Ten Commandments was hung in a Pennsylvania high school, the following note accompanied it: "What an irony that the Ten Commandments are displayed so prominently in the Pennsylvania Supreme Court, yet such displays are prohibited and challenged in classrooms and courthouses across our Nation."

A CONSTITUTIONAL SABBATH

In addition to thousands of displays, the Constitution itself recognizes one of the most religiously specific of the Ten Commandments. In Article I, section 7 of the Constitution, Sunday is set aside as a day of rest for the President, a direct reference to the fourth commandment:

> If any Bill shall not be returned by the President within ten Days (Sundays excepted) after it shall have been presented to him, the Same shall be a Law in like Manner as if he had signed it, unless Congress by their Adjournment prevent its return, in which Case it shall not be a Law.

In addition to the fourth commandment being recognized in the body of the Constitution, the statute books of the states include prohibitions against blasphemy (third), dishonoring parents (fifth), murder (sixth), adultery (seventh), theft (eighth), and perjury (ninth). The fact that the Constitution ends with "in the year of our Lord" certainly reflects the truth of the first commandment: "I am the LORD your God . . . . You shall have no other gods before Me" (Ex. 20:2-3 NASB). The Ten Commandments, from top to bottom, summarize the nature and purpose of law in America by reminding us that neither we nor civil government are God.

WHAT MOSES BROUGHT DOWN FROM MT. SINAI WERE NOT THE TEN SUGGESTIONS. THEY ARE COMMANDMENTS. —TED KOPPEL

CONCLUSION

We cannot live within the fluid boundaries of legal relativism. There must be a definitive and final legal standard of appeal to justify moral decisions at the personal and governmental levels. If not, then one judge's opinion is as good (or as bad) as another. The Ten Commandments has been that fixed standard in America since its founding. As *Nightline* host Ted Koppel stated in a 1987 commencement address at Duke University:

What Moses brought down from Mt. Sinai were not the Ten Suggestions. They are commandments. Are, not were. The sheer brilliance of the Ten Commandments is that they codify in a handful of words acceptable human behavior, not just for then or now, but for all time. Language evolves. Power shifts from one nation to another. Messages are transmitted with the speed of light. Man erases one frontier after another. And yet we and our behavior and the commandments governing that behavior remain the same.[16]

---

[1]De Mille's introductory remarks can be seen only on video and DVD versions of the movie.

[2]Gary DeMar, *Thinking Straight in a Crooked World: A Christian Defense Manual* (Powder Springs, GA: American Vision, 2001).

[3]Archie P. Jones, "Christianity and the First Amendment: The Truth about the Religion Clauses of the Constitution," (unpublished manuscript), 3.

[4]Harry S. Truman, *Harry S. Truman: Public Papers of the Presidents of the United States Containing the Public Messages, Speeches, and Statements of the President*—January 1 to December 31, 1950 (Washington, D.C.: United States Government Printing Office, 1965), 197.

[5]Barbara Reynolds, "If your kids go ape in school, you'll know why," *USA Today* (August 27, 1993), 11A.

[6]C. S. Lewis, *The Abolition of Man* (New York: Macmillan, [1947] 1972), 35.

[7]This story is related by Jabeen Bhatti in "Statue Wars Have Roots in 1950s," *Washington Times* (May 22, 2002). For a more complete story, see "Commanding Presence," *Fraternal Order of Eagles Magazine* (March 2002), 7.

[8]"Commandments back in court," *Atlanta Journal-Constitution* (May 25, 2002), B1.

[9]Rhonda Cook, "ACLU lawsuit puts seal of disapproval on signet," *Atlanta Constitution* (May 16, 2000), A1.

[10]Quoted in Norman Arey, "Ten Commandments display in Ringgold leads ACLU to threaten suit," *Atlanta Journal-Constitution* (October 31, 2001), B1.

[11]Stan Bailey, "Moore puts Commandments monument in court building," *Birmingham News* (August 8, 2001), 1A.

[12]*U.S. Supreme Court Lynch v. Donnelley*, 465 U.S. 668 (decided March 5, 1984), II.C.

[13]David Barton, "The Ten Commandments: A Part of America's Legal System for Almost 400 years!," Prepared and presented in response to multiple ACLU lawsuits against public displays of the Ten Commandments, United States District Court, Eastern District Court, Eastern District of Kentucky, London Division (March 2001).

[14]George Wharton Pepper in Violet Oakley, *The Holy Experiment: Our Heritage from William Penn, 1644-1944* (Philadelphia, PA: Cogslea Studio Productions, 1950), 107. To view all the panels, go to www.courts.state.pa.us/Index/Supreme/indexphotogallery.asp

[15]Oakley, *The Holy Experiment*, 111.

[16]Ted Koppel, "The Last Word," Commencement Address at Duke University, Durham, North Carolina (May 10, 1987). Quoted in Robert H. Bork, *The Tempting of America: The Political Seduction of the Law* (New York: The Free Press, 1989), p. 164.

8

"GOD BLESS AMERICA"

GIVING THANKS TO GOD IN AMERICA

Elias Boudinot

George Washington

"God Bless America" has been reverberating through America since the events of September 11, 2001. A sign on one elementary school, however, caught the attention of passersby. It read, "Bless America." Of course, the first question that comes to mind is, "Who or what are they calling on to bless America?" Is it Aristotle's "Unmoved Mover"? Maybe Allah is to bless us? We should be reminded that the God of the Bible does not share His glory with another, no matter how politically correct the motive:

> I am the LORD, that is My name; and My glory I will not give to another, Nor My praise to carved images (Isaiah 42:8 NKJV; cf. Exodus 20:5; Isaiah 48:11).

As we reflect on Thanksgiving, it would be helpful to retrace the history of this misunderstood and misapplied holiday in light of recent events.

THANKSGIVING BEGINNINGS

On Thursday, September 24, 1789, the First House of Representatives voted to recommend the First Amendment of the newly drafted Constitution to the states for ratification. The next day, New Jersey Congressman Elias Boudinot proposed that the House and Senate jointly request of President Washington to proclaim a day of thanksgiving for "the many signal favors of Almighty God." Boudinot said that he "could not think of letting the session pass over without offering an opportunity to all the citizens of the United States of joining, with one voice, in returning to Almighty God their sincere thanks for the many blessings he had poured down upon them."[1]

Roger Sherman spoke in favor of the proposal by reminding his colleagues that the practice of thanksgiving is "warranted by a number of precedents in holy writ: for instance, the solemn thanksgivings and rejoicings which took place in the time

Roger Sherman

77

of Solomon, after the building of the temple. . . . This example, he thought, worthy of Christian imitation on the present occasion."[2]

A PEOPLE FULL OF THANKSGIVING

The colonists of another era were aware of the many instances of thanksgiving celebrations found in "holy writ." Thanksgiving, as it was practiced by the colonists, was a religious celebration that shared the sentiments of their biblical forerunners, giving thanks to God for His faithful provision, even in times of want. For these devoutly religious people, thanksgiving would have come naturally. "Twice en route the passengers [aboard the *Mayflower*] participated in a fast, and once (two days after sounding ground beneath the *Arabella*) a 'thanksgiving.' When the sailing season ended with all ships accounted for, 'we had a day of thanksgiving in all the plantations.'"[3]

There are numerous claims to the first official Thanksgiving celebrated in the New World. One of the earliest recorded festivals occurred a half century before the Pilgrims landed at Plymouth. "A small colony of French Huguenots established a settlement near present-day Jacksonville, Florida. On June 30, 1564, their leader, René de Laudonnière, recorded that 'We sang a psalm of Thanksgiving unto God, beseeching Him that it would please Him to continue His accustomed goodness towards us.'"[4]

In 1610, after a hard winter called "the starving time," the colonists at Jamestown called for a time of thanksgiving. This was after the original company of 409 colonists had been reduced to 60 survivors. Extreme hardship did not deter the survivors from turning to God in thanksgiving. The colonists prayed for help that finally arrived by a ship filled with food and supplies from England. They held a prayer service to give thanks.

This thanksgiving celebration was not commemorated formally on a yearly basis. An annual commemoration of thanksgiving came nine years later in another part of Virginia. "On December 4, 1619, thirty-eight colonists landed at a place they called Berkeley Hundred [in Virginia]. 'We ordain,' read an instruction in their charter, 'that the day of our ship's arrival . . . in the land of Virginia shall be yearly and perpetually kept holy as a day of Thanksgiving to Almighty God.'"[5]

Edward Winslow

Edward Winslow, in his important chronicle of the history of the Plymouth colony, reports the following eyewitness

"[Y]ET BY THE GOODNESS OF GOD WE ARE SO FAR FROM WANT ..."

—PILGRIM ACCOUNT

account of the colony's thanksgiving celebration:

> Our harvest being gotten in, our governor sent four men on fowling, that so we might, after a special manner, rejoice together after we had gathered the fruit of our labors. They four in one day killed as much fowl as, with a little help beside, served the company almost a week. At which time, among other recreations, we exercised our arms, many of the Indians coming among us, and among the rest their greatest king, Massasoit, with some ninety men, whom for three days we entertained and feasted; and they went out and killed five deer, which they brought to the plantation, and bestowed on our governor, and upon the captain and others. And although it be not always so plentiful as it was at this time with us, *yet by the goodness of God* we are so far from want, that we often wish you partakers of our plenty.[6]

While none of these Thanksgiving celebrations was an official national pronouncement (no nation existed at the time), they do support the claim that the celebrations were religious and specifically Christian in their origin and purpose. "Thanksgiving began as a holy day, created by a community of God-fearing Puritans sincere in their desire to set aside one day each year especially to thank the Lord for His many blessings. The day they chose, coming after the harvest at a time of year when farm work was light, fit the natural rhythm of rural life."[7]

The chain of times set apart for thanksgiving was not even broken during a time of war. Thanksgiving was joined with a spirit of repentance. On October 3, 1863, Abraham Lincoln declared that the last Thursday of November 1863 would be set aside as a nationwide celebration of thanksgiving. His proclamation stated:

Abraham Lincoln

> No human counsel hath devised, nor hath any mortal hand worked out these great things. They are the gracious gifts of the most high God, who, while dealing with us in anger for our sins, hath nevertheless remembered mercy. . . . I do, therefore, invite my fellow citizens in every part of the United States, and those who are sojourning in foreign lands, to set apart and observe the last Thursday in November next as a day of Thanksgiving and praise to our beneficent father who dwelleth in heaven.

Beginning with Lincoln, United States' presidents proclaimed that the last Thursday in November would be set aside for a national day of Thanksgiving. Franklin D. Roosevelt changed the celebration to the third Thursday in November "to give more shopping time between Thanksgiving and Christmas."[8]

The erosion of the original intent of Thanksgiving, as it was practiced by the colonists and sanctioned by presidents and Congress, can best be illustrated by the way some textbooks handle the subject. One elementary school social studies book has thirty pages of material "on the Pilgrims, including the first Thanksgiving. But there is not one word (or image) that referred to religion as even a part of the Pilgrims' life. One mother whose son is in a class using this book wrote . . . that he came home and told her that 'Thanksgiving was when the Pilgrims gave thanks to the Indians.' The mother called the principal of this suburban New York City school to point out that Thanksgiving was when the Pilgrims thanked God. The principal responded by saying 'that was her opinion'—the schools could only teach what was in the books!"[9]

There is no doubt that these early Christian settlers thanked the Indians for their generosity in supplying venison to supplement the Pilgrims' meager Thanksgiving rations of parsnips, carrots, turnips, onions, radishes, and beets

from their household gardens. As the historical record shows, however, thanksgiving was ultimately made to the God of the Bible. "Governor Bradford, with one eye on divine Providence, proclaimed a day of thanksgiving to God, and with the other eye on the local political situation, extended an invitation to neighboring Indians to share in the harvest feast. . . . This 'first Thanksgiving' was a feast called to suit the needs of the hour, which were to celebrate the harvest, thank the Lord for His goodness, and regale and impress the Indians."[10]

Early celebrations of thanksgiving were expressions of deep gratitude to God for life itself. Many who partook of the bounty from God's creation set before them were thankful just to be alive. How times have changed in America.

---

[1]*The Annals of the Congress*, The Debates and Proceedings in the Congress of the United States, Compiled From Authentic Materials by Joseph Gales, Senior (Washington, DC: Gales and Seaton, 1834), 1:949-50.

[2]*Annals of the Congress*, 950.

[3]David D. Hall, *Worlds of Wonder, Days of Judgment: Popular Religious Belief in Early New England* (New York: Alfred A. Knopf, 1989), 166.

[4]Diana Karter Appelbaum, *Thanksgiving: An American Holiday, An American History* (New York: Facts on File Publications, 1984), 14-15.

[5]Jim Dwyer, ed., *Strange Stories, Amazing Facts of America's Past* (Pleasantville, NY: The Reader's Digest Association, Inc., 1989), 198.

[6]Edward Winslow, *How the Pilgrim Fathers Lived*, 2:116. Emphasis added. CD Sourcebook of American History (Mesa, AR: Candlelight Publishing, 1992). Also see *Mourt's Relation: A Journal of the Pilgrims of Plymouth*, ed. Jordan D. Fiore (Plymouth, MA: Plymouth Rock Foundation, [1622] 1985), 67-69.

[7]Appelbaum, *Thanksgiving*, 186. The celebration of Christmas, in addition to Thanksgiving, has become an ordeal in censorship. "Silent Night" and other sacred songs have been stripped from public school Christmas pageants and replaced with "Jingle Bells" and "Frosty the Snowman." Public school officials and school teachers are made to substitute "winter holiday" for Christmas. In St. Paul Minnesota, an affirmative action officer for the state tax department, banned what she called the "unwelcome greeting of Merry Christmas" via the department's electronic mail. ("'Merry Christmas' offense, bureaucrat rules," Atlanta Journal/Constitution [December 11, 1994], A11).

[8]Edmund H. Harvey, Jr., ed., *Readers Digest Book of Facts* (Pleasantville, NY: The Reader's Digest Association, [1985] 1987), 125.

[9]Paul C. Vitz, *Censorship: Evidence of Bias in Our Children's Textbooks* (Ann Arbor, MI: Servant Books, 1986), 3.

[10]Appelbaum, *Thanksgiving*, 9.

CONCLUSION

GOD GOVERNS IN THE AFFAIRS OF MEN

William McGuffey

With so many original historical sources available, and with so much evidence in, why is it that most Americans are unaware of their rich Christian heritage? Much of the blame needs to be laid at the school door, although the fault is not usually with the teacher. History textbooks are almost uniformly lacking in any mention of the large role that the Christian religion played in the founding and development of this great nation. This is true from the earliest grades through high school and college.

A study of America's early textbooks reveals that religion played a major role in the development of the public school curriculum. "Textbooks referred to God without embarrassment, and public schools considered one of their major tasks to be the development of character through the teaching of religion. For example, the New England Primer opened with religious admonitions followed by the Lord's Prayer, the Apostles' Creed, the Ten Commandments, and the names of the books of the Bible."[1]

The most widely used textbook series used in public schools from 1836 to 1920 were William Holmes McGuffey's *Eclectic Readers*. More than 120 million *Readers* were sold during this period. The *Readers* stressed religion and its relationship to morality and the proper use of knowledge. In the introduction to a reprint edition of the *Fifth Reader*, historian Henry Steele Commager writes:

> What was the nature of the morality that permeated the *Readers*? It was deeply religious, and . . . religion then meant a Protestant Christianity. . . . The world of the *McGuffeys* was a world where no one questioned the truths of the Bible or their relevance to everyday contact. . . . The *Readers*, therefore, are filled with stories from the Bible, and tributes to its truth and beauty.[2]

Competing textbooks of the same era contained varying amounts of biblical material, but *McGuffey* contained the greatest amount—"more than three times as much as any other text of the period."[3] Subsequent editions of the

Readers—1857 and 1879—showed a reduction in the amount of material devoted to biblical material. Even so, the 1879 edition contained the Sermon on the Mount, two selections from the Book of Psalms, the Lord's Prayer, the story of the death of Absalom (2 Sam. 18), and Paul's speech on the Areopagus (Acts 17). The Bible was still referred to as "'the Book of God,' 'a source of inspiration,' 'an important basis for life,' and was cited in support of particular moral issues."[4]

ANTISEPTIC TEXTS

For some time secular historians have steadily chipped away at the historical record, denying the impact Christianity had on the moral and political character of the United States. In 1898 Bishop Charles Galloway delivered a series of messages in the Chapel at Emory College in Georgia. He noted that "books on the making of our nation have been written, and are the texts in our colleges, in which the Christian religion, as a social and civil factor, has only scant or apologetic mention. This is either a fatal oversight or a deliberate purpose, and both alike to be deplored and condemned. A nation ashamed of its ancestry will be despised by its posterity."[5]

In more recent years there has been an even greater dilution of the historical record. So much so that even the liberal group, People for the American Way had to acknowledge that religion is often overlooked in history textbooks: "Religion is simply not treated as a significant element in American life—it is not portrayed as an integrated part of the American value system or as something that is important to individual Americans."[6] A study of history textbooks commissioned by the federal government and drafted by the National Center for History in the Schools at UCLA concluded that religion "was foolishly purged from many recent textbooks."[7] In 1990, Warren A. Nord of the University of North Carolina wrote:

What cannot be doubted is that our ways of thinking about nature, morality, art, and society were once (and for many people still are) fundamentally religious, and still today in our highly secular world it is difficult even for the non-religious to extricate themselves entirely from the webs of influence and meaning provided by our religious past. . . . To understand history and (historical) literature one must understand a great deal about religion: on this all agree. Consequently, the relative absence of religion from history textbooks is deeply troubling.[8]

It seems that every image and word of America's Christian heritage is being wiped clean. The day may come when biblical place names like Bethlehem, Smyrna, and Zion will have no meaning. This is no exaggeration. The Federal appeals court in Chicago declared that the city seal of Zion, Illinois, was unconstitutional. The seal displays a banner with the words "God Reigns" surrounded by images of a dove, a cross, a sword, and a crown.

Corporate Seal of the city of Zion, Illinois

Will the day come when no one knows the meaning of Zion? We are a nation that has lost its historical memory.

WE HAVE NOW FORGOTTEN

On June 28, 1787, Benjamin Franklin made a powerful and stirring speech to the those in attendance at the Constitutional Convention in Philadelphia. His words then are no less true today. In fact, they strike a profound prophetic note that serve as a disturbing warning to all who would dismiss God's providential hand in the establishment and maintenance of the United States of America:

> All of us who were engaged in the struggle [in the war for independence] must have observed frequent instances of a superintending Providence in our favor. To that kind Providence we owe this happy opportunity of consulting in peace on the means of establishing our future national felicity. And have we now forgotten that powerful Friend? Or do we imagine we no longer need His assistance? I have lived . . . a long time, and the longer I live, the more convincing proofs I see of this truth—that God Governs in the affairs of men. And if a sparrow cannot fall to the ground without His

notice,[9] is it probable that an empire can rise without His aid? We have been assured, sir, in the Sacred Writings, that 'except the Lord build the house, they labor in vain that build it.'[10] I firmly believe this; and I also believe that without His concurring aid we shall succeed in this political building no better than the builders of Babel.

Benjamin Franklin

It's not too late to recover our nation's Christian past. Of course, it takes more than resurrecting dust laden history texts. There must be a renewed spirit to reestablish what has been forgotten and lost so "that the generation to come might know, even the children yet to be born, that they may arise and tell them to their children, that they should put their confidence in God, and not forget the works of God, but keep His commandments" (Psalm 78:6-7 NASB).

[1] John W. Whitehead, *The Rights of Religious Persons in Public Education: A Complete Resource for Knowing and Exercising Your Rights in Public Education*, rev. ed. (Wheaton, IL: Crossway Books, [1991] 1994), 41-42.

[2] Henry Steele Commager, Preface, *McGuffey's Fifth Eclectic Reader*. Quoted in Whitehead, *The Rights of Religious Persons in Public Education*, 42.

[3] John H. Westerhoff, III, "The Struggle for a Common Culture: Biblical Images in Nineteenth-Century Schoolbooks," *The Bible in American Education*, eds. David L. Barr and Nicholas Piediscalzi (Philadelphia, PA: Fortress Press, 1982), 32.

[4] Westerhoff, "The Struggle for a Common Culture: Biblical Images in Nineteenth-Century Schoolbooks," 28.

[5] Charles B. Galloway, *Christianity and the American Commonwealth; or, The Influence of Christianity in Making This Nation* (Nashville, TN: Methodist Episcopal Church, 1898), 15.

[6] O. L. Davis, Jr., et al., *Looking at History: A Review of Major U.S. History Textbooks* (1986), 3. Quoted in Joan Delfattore, *What Johnny Shouldn't Read: Textbook Censorship in America* (New Haven, CT: Yale University Press, 1992), 85.

[7] This is the conclusion of the editorial writers of the *Marietta Daily Journal*: "History needing revision" (October 30, 1994), 2D. The National Standards for United States History have called for the restoration of the role religion played in the founding of America while pushing a "politically correct" agenda in nearly everything else. See Lynne V. Cheney, "The End of History," *Wall Street Journal* (October 20, 1994), A24.

[8] Warren A. Nord, "Taking Religion Seriously," Social Education, vol. 54, no. 9 (September 1990), 287. Quoted in *History Textbooks: A Standard and Guide*, 1994-95 Edition (New York: American Textbook Council, 1994), 32.

[9] Matthew 10:29.

[10] Psalm 127:1.

EPILOGUE

The evidence is in. America was indeed founded as a Christian nation, as Gary DeMar so ably demonstrates. From Plymouth Rock to Independence Hall and beyond, the record is replete with evidence that ours is a nation deeply rooted in Christianity.

From the first Charter of Virginia that spoke of "propagating of the Christian religion to such people, as yet live in darkness," to Harvard College that "laid Christ at the bottom," to the U.S. Constitution that was approved in the "year of our Lord" 1787, to federal proclamations of prayer and thanksgiving to God, there is abundant testimony for the claim that America was founded by Christians to be a biblical "city on a hill."

As the Supreme Court concluded in 1892, "this is a Christian nation."

But much has changed since then. In the last 50 years, our nation has drifted from the biblical moorings on which America was built. So much so, that the mere assertion that ours is a Christian nation invites an argument from academic and media elites. Today, Americans have largely forgotten— or never learned—about the profound and deeply embedded role of biblical Christianity in America's rise from a colony of Britain to the mightiest nation on earth.

How we lost our moorings and our drift into moral relativism and culture-wide amnesia as to our nation's religious heritage is powerfully addressed in *America Adrift*, the second volume in Coral Ridge Ministries' American Destiny Series.

I sincerely hope that *America's Christian Heritage* has aided your understanding of our nation's wonderful Christian heritage, a treasure which DeMar and others are unearthing in our time.

—*D. James Kennedy*
Senior Minister
Coral Ridge Presbyterian Church